THE FLY FISHING LEGACY OF T C IVENS

RESERVOIR NYMPH PATTERNS, TECHNIQUES AND TACKLE INNOVATIONS BY TOM IVENS

*T C Ivens at Seale-Hayne
Agricultural College in 1952*
Image courtesy of The Seale-Haynians
(Alumni) Club

'No one had more influence on the development of reservoir fishing than T C Ivens with the publication in 1952 of his *Still Water Fly-Fishing* which went through at least four editions and was reprinted several times.'

Conrad Voss Bark

THE FLY FISHING LEGACY OF T C IVENS

Reservoir Nymph Patterns, Techniques and Tackle Innovations by Tom Ivens

Adrian V W Freer

wcp

Welford Court Press

The Fly Fishing Legacy of T C Ivens: Reservoir Nymph Patterns, Techniques and Tackle Innovations by Tom Ivens

Fly Fishing Heritage Series: Number Two

Welford Court Press
4 Whitebeam Road
Oadby
Leicester LE2 4EA
United Kingdom
www.webdatauk.wixsite.com/welford-court-press

Distributed by Amazon Fulfilment

© Adrian V W Freer 2021

All rights reserved. No part of this publication may be reproduced, stored in a retrieval system, recorded or transmitted by any means without permission from the publishers.

First published 2021
First Edition

British Library Cataloguing-in-Publication Data
A catalogue record for this book is available from the British Library.

ISBN: 978-0-9520304-3-0

Dedication: To my wife, Louise, for her encouragement during my fishing forays, for taking some of the photographs, and her invaluable assistance with my literary efforts.

Cover illustration: Tom Ivens with a four-fish limit of Hollowell Reservoir trout [Image courtesy of the Ivens family].

CONTENTS

	Page
Acknowledgements	6
Illustrations	7
Preface	10
1 Biography of T C Ivens	12
2 Impact of the publication of *Still Water Fly-Fishing*	21
3 Traditional flies, deceivers and flashers	26
4 Distance casting and retrieve methods	33
5 Fly dressing	37
6 T C Ivens' original (1952) series of fly patterns	41
7 Ravensthorpe Reservoir and Hollowell Reservoir	53
8 T C Ivens' second (1970/75) series of fly patterns	57
9 Grafham Water	71
10 T C Ivens' river patterns	73
11 References to T C Ivens	79
12 Progress of reservoir fly fishing	83
13 Fishing tackle innovations by T C Ivens	88
14 Books and articles written by T C Ivens	91
15 Postscript	92
Notes	95
Bibliography	97
The Author	99
Index	100
Dr Bell of Wrington	102

Notes to the text appear after chapter fifteen

ACKNOWLEDGEMENTS

The author would like to take this opportunity to record his grateful appreciation to all those who have contributed towards the creation of this present volume; without their valuable assistance it would not be as comprehensive as it is. It has been a continual source of encouragement that many of those contacted have willingly responded to requests for help and shared my enthusiasm.

Tom Ivens' family have kindly granted permission to include several photographs of him and their agreement is gratefully acknowledged.

I would also like to offer thanks to the following organisations and people who have given permission to reproduce material previously published by them or to which they hold the rights: Bonhams Auctions, The Crowood Press, *Fly Fishing & Fly Tying* magazine, Merlin Unwin Books, The Seale-Haynians (Alumni) Club, Thanetcraft Ltd, Welbeck Publishing, The Wrington Archive, Colin Brett, Simon Daligan, Adam Fox-Edwards, Brian Harris, Bob Meadows and Steve Taylor.

Many people have supplied invaluable information that has helped my research into this fascinating pioneer of reservoir fly angling including Charlie Abrahams, Raymond Bartlett, Bob Draper, Stuart East and David Rowe of Anglian Water, Grafham Water Fly Fishers' Association, Seumas Halliday, Julie Ivens, Miriam Ivens, Neil Ivens, Richard Ivens, Ifor Jones, The Mid-Northants Trout Fishers' Association, Donald Moore and John Wadham. I would like to express my deep gratitude to them all for their time, assistance and kind forbearance.

I am once again indebted to Helen Ives for conducting a considerable amount of painstaking genealogical research, a subject outside my area of expertise, which has filled in many of the gaps of what we know about Tom Ivens.

Finally I would like to record my deep and sincere gratitude to my wife, Louise, for her support, patience and encouragement during my literary endeavours, and for reading and commenting on the numerous drafts and re-drafts of this book.

ILLUSTRATIONS

T C Ivens at Seale-Hayne Agricultural College in 1952   Frontispiece

Preface
T C Ivens' Black & Peacock Spider and Jersey Herd   10
Rare image of T C Ivens fishing at Two Lakes in Hampshire 11

Chapter 1
Tom Ivens in his late-twenties   12
North Block and Quad at Seale-Hayne Agricultural College   13
Phalaenopsis lueddemanniana   14
Tom Ivens in later years   15
First edition of *Still Water Fly-Fishing*   16
'Superflyte' Shooting Head   17
Notable locations in the life of T C Ivens   19
T C Ivens (1921-1988)   20

Chapter 2
Corixa patterns designed and tied by Arthur Cove   21
The Bell: a noted 'hotspot' at Eyebrook Reservoir   22
Cyril Inwood (1911-1971)   24

Chapter 3
Loch Leven, Scotland   26
Rare image of Dr Bell of Wrington taken in 1945   28
Ravensthorpe Reservoir in Northamptonshire   30
Tom Ivens with a 12½lb Border Esk salmon   31

Chapter 4
Bank fishing at Eyebrook Reservoir   33
Extracts from the double-haul casting sequence   34
Table: Recovery speeds converted to seconds per foot   36

Chapter 5
Bell's Bug, Sawyer's Killer Bug and Ivens' Gentile   38
Dr Bell's Blagdon Buzzer Nymph and T C Ivens' Black Buzzer 38
Hackle configurations   39
Table: Conversion table of hook sizes   40

Chapter 6
Evening fishing at Hollowell Reservoir, c.1950s 41
Flies from T C Ivens' original (1952) series of flies 42
Black & Peacock Spider 43
Tandem Black & Peacock Spider 44
Green Nymph 45
Brown Nymph 46
Green & Yellow Nymph 47
Brown & Green Nymph 48
Pretty Pretty 49
Jersey Herd 50
Alexandra 51
Fuzzy Buzzy 52

Chapter 7
Angler's map of Ravensthorpe Reservoir 53
Ravensthorpe Reservoir 54
Angler's map of Hollowell Reservoir 55
Hollowell Reservoir 56

Chapter 8
Bank fishing in Pig's Bay, Grafham Water 57
T C Ivens' second (1970/75) series of flies 58
Gentile 59
Buzzer 60
Autopsy disclosing dozens of black buzzer pupae 61
Cinnamon & Gold 62
Polar Bear 63
Black Knight 64
Hair Wing Butcher 65
Daddy Long Legs 66
Black Knight Tandem Streamer 67
Whisky Fly 68
Muddler Minnow 69
Sticky Willy 70

Chapter 9
Angler's map of Grafham Water 71

Sunrise at Grafham Water   72

Chapter 10
G E M Skues' Olive Nymph   73
Pheasant Tail   74
March Brown   75
Partridge & Orange   76
Olive Yellow Nymph   77
Green Nymph (River Version)   78

Chapter 11
A History of Flyfishing   79
Fly Fishing & Fly Tying   80
Fishing for Lake Trout   81
Reservoir Trout Flies   82

Chapter 12
Stocking with takeable size fish at Eyebrook Reservoir   83
Two-at-a-time for the author!   85
The black peril!   87

Chapter 13
'Farstrike' T C Ivens Ravensthorpe 9ft 4in split-cane fly rod   88
The *'Stillwater'* fishing boat   90

Chapter 14
Four editions of *Still Water Fly-Fishing*   91

Chapter 15
Blagdon Lake and the fishing lodge   92
Tom Ivens with a four-fish limit of Hollowell trout   94

Appendices
The Author   99
Dr Bell of Wrington   102

Unless otherwise stated in the text all flies are tied by the author.

PREFACE

The development of reservoir fly fishing in England has produced a number of truly great innovators who laid the foundations of stillwater fly fishing today. Among those who made significant contributions were the legendary Dr Bell of Wrington, Geoffrey Bucknall, Richard Walker, Dick Shrive and Arthur Cove; and within that select company must surely be included T C Ivens.

Tom Ivens fished Ravensthorpe Reservoir and Hollowell Reservoir in the immediate post-WW2 years and during that time he made many ground-breaking advances that have changed the way that fly anglers fish forever. It is impossible to over-emphasize the influence he had on the progress of the sport which largely came as a result of the publication of *Still Water Fly-Fishing* in 1952. The ideas he proposed were truly revolutionary and quickly became the benchmark for tackling reservoirs and lakes.

T C Ivens' Black & Peacock Spider and Jersey Herd

What sets Tom Ivens apart from his contemporaries is the fact that he endeavoured to adopt a scientific, *thinking* approach rather than slavishly follow the traditional methods that were being used by the majority of anglers.

The innovations he introduced were considerable and touched every aspect of tackle and technique but he is probably best known for the design of two series of fly patterns which became extremely popular at the time. His Black & Peacock Spider and Jersey Herd are probably two of the most widely used artificial flies to this day. In addition he designed a range of reservoir fly rods, a series of shooting head fly lines and a range of single- and double-tapered nylon monofilament leader profiles. All these will be covered in the following chapters and looking at the long list Tom Ivens was extremely prolific in his achievements.

Many well-known angling writers have taken to print to pay tribute to the innovations that Tom Ivens introduced: Conrad Voss Bark, Geoffrey Bucknall (both of whom are quoted here), C F Walker, David J Collyer, Kenneth Robson, Arthur Cove and Taff Price amongst them (the list is again a long one). Having said that, and for reasons best known to themselves, a few authors strangely make no mention of him whatever. Whether this is deliberate or an oversight one can but surmise. Nevertheless it is actions and not words (or the lack of them) that have the final say and thousands of his rods were sold, millions of his flies have been tied, and multiple millions of trout have been landed over the years as a result of the advances introduced by this one man.

Rare image of T C Ivens fishing at Two Lakes in Hampshire
Image courtesy of Brian Harris

In view of the tremendous impact he had on stillwater fly fishing in England it is somewhat surprising to note that there is little biographical information about Tom Ivens in the public domain. That being the case it was decided to write this present volume in order that the legacy of this outstanding angler is preserved for posterity. To complement this book a website dedicated to him has been created and there is a Wikipedia entry in his name in order that information about him is accessible online. It is hoped that together they will provide a fitting memorial to a remarkable man who has inspired many rewarding fishing hours at the waterside for countless millions of stillwater fly anglers, not only in England but worldwide.

In addition, by looking at his accomplishments it enables us to better understand just how radically and rapidly (in angling terms) the sport of stillwater fly fishing has progressed in recent times.

Adrian V W Freer
Leicester 2021

Chapter 1

BIOGRAPHY OF TOM IVENS

Although he must undoubtedly rank amongst the greatest innovators in the sport of fly fishing, with one of the bestselling books on the subject to his name, facts about the life of T C Ivens are somewhat sketchy. The details that follow have been culled from a variety of sources and it is hoped that they will enable readers to understand a little more about this fascinating, and at times controversial, character in the history of angling.

THE EARLY YEARS

Thomas Coleman Ivens (1921–1988) was born, one of three children, to Thomas Edward Ivens and Ella Rosina Ivens (née Richards) in Northampton on the 22nd May 1921. His early school years were spent studying at Northampton Grammar School.

In 1941 he married Ruth Joan Walden (1922-2003) at St Stephen's Church in her home city of Gloucester and they were to have three children. She was later to draw the illustrations for his books.

As a young man Tom Ivens joined The Royal Navy during WW2 and in 1942 he is listed as serving on *HMS St Angelo* (Malta), in 1943 on *ML 135*, and from 1944 until 1947 he was Commanding Officer of Royal Navy minesweepers.

Tom Ivens in his late-twenties
Image courtesy of the Ivens family

COLLEGE YEARS

In 1950, at the age of 29, he enrolled at Seale-Hayne Agricultural College, Newton Abbott, in Devon where he studied until 1952 for the college diploma, The Science and Practice of Agriculture (CDA) and also The National Diploma in Agriculture (NDA). The diploma course had been three years before WW2 but with so many men being called up and the urgent need to replace them it was contracted into a two-year intensive course.

In 1989 the college merged with Plymouth Polytechnic to form the Seale-Hayne Faculty of Agriculture and afterwards it became part of the University of Plymouth in 1992. It finally closed in 2005.

North Block and Quad at Seale-Hayne Agricultural College
Image courtesy of Simon Daligan

Although Tom Ivens grew up in Northampton, he lived in various parts of the country during his lifetime including Dover, Surrey, Skipton, Hemel Hempstead and St Albans. He finally returned to Northamptonshire to live in Pitsford village and last of all Moulton.

According to those who knew or met him Tom Ivens was a polite, courteous and unassuming man who had a good grasp of words which certainly comes across in his writing. He also had other interests apart from fly fishing which included photography, orchid growing, jazz, football and his family life was important to him.

ORCHIDS

Tom Ivens worked as a project manager for Sir Robert McAlpine & Sons Ltd, builders, but his passion for orchids led to him raising them firstly as a leisure pursuit and then cultivating them on a commercial basis and in due course founding Ivens Orchids Ltd in 1970. The company specialised in the production of *phalaenopsis* and *cymbidiums* for the cut bloom florist trade.

Phalaenopsis lueddemanniana
Public domain image

The Ivens Orchids nursery was situated on a 1,280 square metre site at Great Barn Dell, St Albans Road, Sandridge in Hertfordshire and it was there that Tom Ivens had the foresight to raise some of the rarest orchids, some of which were available nowhere else. It held one of the oldest orchids, the *Calanthe Baron Schroder* dating back to 1894, produced by Frederick Sanders one of the earliest orchid collectors of the 1880s.

The business was eventually sold to the Cook family as a going concern in 1987 but it continued to trade under the Ivens name.

RESERVOIR FLY FISHING

Tom Ivens is best known for his contribution to reservoir fly fishing. After the hostilities of WW2 had ceased he resumed the sport which he had practiced before the war, regularly fishing Ravensthorpe Reservoir and Hollowell Reservoir, both of which were at that time stocked with trout. In the late 1950s Hollowell suffered an infestation by pike and as a result it became a coarse fishery. From time to time he also fished Durleigh Reservoir and Chew Valley Lake in Somerset. It was during this time that he devised and honed his flies and methods which he described in a series of articles in *Fishing Gazette* in 1951 entitled *Reservoir Trout Fishing*. They were to form the basis of his book *Still Water Fly-Fishing*.

RESERVOIR FLY PATTERNS

Tom Ivens' approach to fly selection was based on the premise that no matter how accurate are the fly-dresser's attempts at 'exact imitation' of the trout's natural food, they will always fall short, in both form and movement, of closely replicating the natural creatures present in reservoirs.

He considered that employing 'attractor' patterns which give the impression of life and of being food, but do not specifically imitate any food item in particular, will prove to be the most successful tactic.

Most of his flies are nymph-like 'deceiver' representations that need to be recovered slowly to complete the deception and he recommended that they should be used whenever the conditions allowed. He also designed several 'flasher' patterns for those occasions when the wind and weather conditions were such that the use of slowly moving flies was impractical. His Jersey Herd pattern remains one of the most popular lures to this day.

Tom Ivens in later years
Image courtesy of the Ivens family

A few of his second set of flies are, however, somewhat more imitative in their construction than those of his original series. His Buzzer pattern is a passable representation of the natural creature (it also bears a close resemblance to the Blagdon Buzzer Nymph designed by Dr Bell of Wrington which was created a generation earlier) and he produced a close-copy imitation of the Daddy Long Legs (or Crane Fly).

PUBLICATION OF *STILL WATER FLY-FISHING*

Tom Ivens' first and only full-length angling book, *Still Water Fly-Fishing*, quickly became a bestseller and it extended to four editions. The book grew larger with each revision as new information was incorporated (the first edition consisted of 128 pages and the fourth edition ran to 319 pages) but the overall strategy remained very much unaltered throughout. It is considered by many to be an angling 'classic' and essential reading for every fly angler to this day.

First edition of Still Water Fly-Fishing
Image courtesy of Welbeck Publishing

He also contributed several pieces to anthologies and wrote numerous articles for a variety of fishing magazines (listed in chapter fourteen).

He was appointed secretary of the Mid-Northants Trout Fishers' Association at its inception in 1952 which was formed to represent angling interests with the Mid-Northamptonshire Water Board.

Shortly after the publication of *Still Water Fly-Fishing* he was appointed to the staff of *Fishing Gazette* in 1953 where he remained until 1956.

SKIRMISHES WITH RICHARD WALKER

It has been suggested that Tom Ivens and Richard Walker did not get along with one another – presumably as a result of their sparring in the columns of the angling journals (it has to be said that Dick Walker enjoyed nothing more than a bit of controversy when it suited him and it did provoke interest, and no doubt sales, in the magazines). That was not the case and whilst they could not be described as being the closest of friends, they nevertheless did have a warm and respectful relationship and they exchanged correspondence with one another on a variety of angling topics.

At one time Richard Walker had described Ivens' long distance casting methods as nothing more than *'bone-headed athleticism'* but once Grafham Water had opened near to Walker's home he adopted those self-same methods himself to reach the fish there. Although Walker wrote about long-distance casting many times it is regrettable that he did not give Tom Ivens the credit that he deserved (an omission that Geoffrey Bucknall sought to remedy in the article reproduced in chapter eleven).

FISHING TACKLE DESIGN AND METHODS

Tom Ivens was at the forefront in the design of the new fly fishing techniques and tackle that were crucial in order to catch reservoir trout from the bank and his innovations encompassed many diverse facets.

He popularized the double-haul casting technique which was employed in conjunction with a double-taper fly line for maximum distance and the minimum disturbance of the water in order not to alarm the trout.

'Superflyte' Shooting Head

He designed an extensive range of split-cane and fibre-glass fishing rods that were specifically intended for long distance casting on reservoirs (these were marketed by Davenport & Fordham Ltd – I still have my *'Farstrike'* T C Ivens Ravensthorpe 9ft 4in split-cane fly rod weighing in at 6.35oz and it is a beautifully hand-crafted piece of equipment). He also designed the *'Superflyte'* range of shooting head fly lines as well as a reservoir wading landing net.

In the area of terminal tackle he introduced a series of single- and double-tapered nylon monofilament leader profiles that were capable of turning the flies over correctly under a wide range of wind and weather conditions.

Tom Ivens' achievements did not end there. In 1968 he was engaged as a consultant in the design of the *'Stillwater'* fishing boat manufactured by Thanetcraft, at that time of New Malden in Surrey.

The technical specifications of all these innovations will be described in chapter thirteen.

RIVER TROUT, SEA-TROUT AND SALMON

Less well documented is Tom Ivens' involvement in river fly fishing for trout, sea-trout and salmon where he adopted the same reasoned 'thinking' approach that he applied to reservoirs.

A comprehensive article detailing the flies, equipment and methods necessary to tackle a variety of river situations throughout the season appeared under the title *River Trouting with the Sunken Fly* in the three-volume *The Art of Angling*. In it he recorded that he found that his reservoir nymphs were just as successful on rivers as they were on still water and to complement them he designed five new patterns specifically intended for river trout. These will be described in detail in a later chapter.

AQUACULTURE

As a result of his agricultural studies Tom Ivens possessed an extensive knowledge of fish biology, genetics and the aquatic environment that trout inhabit which he put to good use in his fishing excursions. His article, *The Biology of the Trout,* published in *The Art of Angling,* is a concise introduction to our quarry that all fly fishers would benefit from studying.

In his writings he is at great pains to explain that still waters vary widely and that they are in fact rarely still but rather constantly moving bodies of water and understanding them better helps anglers in their attempts to catch the trout that reside there. Amongst the significant factors that anglers need to take into account are the location of lakes which dictates the amount of natural food available to the fish[1], wind and wave action which influences the way in which the fish behave, and seasonal migrations that account for where the trout are likely to be found at different times of the year. He maintained that having an accurate grasp of all these aspects is vital if the angler is to make the most of his fishing opportunities. As a result of his wide-ranging knowledge of aquaculture, Tom Ivens acted as a consultant to several fisheries in the formulation of their stocking policy.

By his own admission, and somewhat surprisingly in view of his understanding of fish biology, Tom Ivens did not possess a deep interest in entomology which is a shame because with his scientific background his insights would doubtless have been worth hearing.

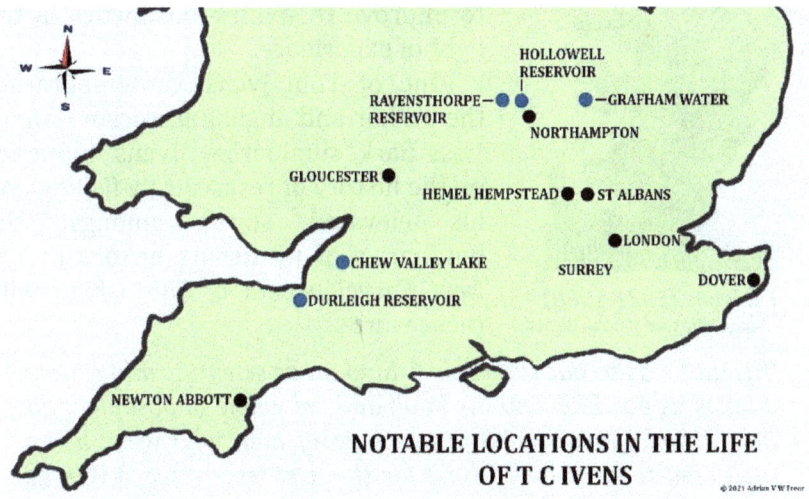

NOTABLE LOCATIONS IN THE LIFE OF T C IVENS

LATER YEARS AND DEATH

John Wadham recounts an amusing incident that occurred in July 1976 when he was fishing with some success from the dam wall at Grafham Water. A nearby angler, who he did not know, walked up to enquire what fly he was using and John gave him a couple of the successful pattern, which was an Ivens' Brown & Green Nymph. Within fifteen minutes the other angler had a bend in his rod and from that point on they were both catching fish regularly. When they came together later it transpired that the other angler was in fact Tom Ivens and John had presented him with a couple of his own patterns which Tom had graciously accepted and put to good use!

In his later years Tom Ivens moved to a bungalow in Pitsford village next to the reservoir of that name and one of his favourite fishing spots there was at Pitsford Creek which was just a short distance from his home. He was a close friend of the renowned Northampton fly dresser, Cyril Lineham, and during this time they spent many hours together experimenting with new patterns which goes to show that even the most celebrated of fly fishers continually seek to improve their flies and tactics in the light of experience.

T C Ivens (1921-1988)
Image courtesy of Brian Harris

One of Tom Ivens' contemporaries, the author and angling historian Conrad Voss Bark, summarized Ivens' influence on the history of reservoir fly fishing and his elevated status amongst the luminaries of fly fishing history in *The New Encyclopaedia of Fly Fishing* with these words:

'His aim was to put reservoir fishing on as scientific and simple a basis as possible, and his book and his whole philosophy had an instant appeal to large numbers of men who were being attracted to reservoir fishing for the first time since WWII, as well as those who had previously been fishing traditional wet flies without knowing quite why.'

Tom Ivens finally moved to a bungalow at Moulton, on the northern outskirts of Northampton. He died of leukaemia in Northampton General Hospital on the 9th July 1988 at the relatively young age of 67. He was buried in Northampton and was survived by his wife, Ruth, and his three children: Elizabeth, Roger and James.

Despite his early demise his ultimate legacy, that of the millions of reservoir fly anglers worldwide who are to this day still using the flies and techniques that he devised many decades ago, nonetheless lives on.

Chapter 2

IMPACT OF THE PUBLICATION OF
STILL WATER FLY-FISHING

The 1940s and 1950s saw an increase in interest in stillwater trout fishing with the opening of Eyebrook, Ladybower and other reservoirs to fly anglers who had previously only fished rivers, and also coarse fishermen during the coarse fishing close season. These anglers were confronted with a host of new problems that they had not encountered before: what tackle to choose, how to cast a long fly line, what flies to employ, how the flies needed to be recovered and so on. In the normal course of events they would turn to their more experienced 'brothers of the angle' for advice but sometimes that help was not always as forthcoming as perhaps it ought to have been as the following accounts by well-known anglers all too sadly demonstrate.

Corixa patterns designed and tied by Arthur Cove

Arthur Cove recounted an incident that occurred at Eyebrook Reservoir during his early fly fishing career when, as a raw beginner, he was not very successful. He had observed a nearby angler catch a nice brace of fish and walked a hundred yards along the bank to ask him what was his successful fly. In response the angler promptly hid his flies tightly in the palm of his hand and told him to find out, the same as he had done[2]. Fly fishing is not an easy craft to master and such an attitude is not helpful to beginners.

Bob Church tells of an occurrence, also at Eyebrook Reservoir, when Cyril Inwood (who incidentally gave Tom Ivens his first casting lesson with a fly rod in 1937) was catching whilst everyone else was fishless. When asked what fly he was using he replied that it was a claret nymph. With that everyone tried a claret fly, again without success. It came to light that this was a deception when it was discovered that the fly in question was in fact pillar-box red and not claret[3]. Inwood passed the ruse off with the rejoinder *'I must be colour blind.'* Life is surely too short for such duplicity[4].

Alan Pearson makes the point in *Trout Angler's Angles* that information about what fly is being used and how it is presented should be given freely and with goodwill in response to a polite request because that is nothing more than good angling etiquette[5].

The Bell (centre): a noted 'hotspot' at Eyebrook Reservoir

He nevertheless concludes somewhat ruefully that *'if the information is not forthcoming, then you are dealing with either a very rude angler, or possibly one who has been trained in the Northampton school never to divulge anything at all.'*

ENCOURAGING NEWCOMERS

An episode that sticks in my mind from my early fly fishing days concerns an afternoon at Ravensthorpe Reservoir. A couple of anglers had returned to the jetty with a few fish in the bag and I asked them politely what flies had been successful. My request was initially met with a tight-lipped silence but, when pressed, I was grudgingly told that it was a *'black and green thing'* – that is all they would divulge. That was unkind to a novice who was muddling through and had no one to turn to for advice. As a result of that experience I resolved, and have adhered to that pledge, that if I managed to be successful I would be totally open with whatever information was requested and whenever the opportunity presented itself offer a couple of flies to the enquirer. Those of us who tie our own flies have far more than we will ever use and apart from the few minutes of time it costs us nothing – but such help can be of immense encouragement to the recipient.

On those (few) occasions when I manage to do well when others are struggling I make a point of writing something that could be of help in the returns log. A few words such as 'Green Bay/Buzzers/ slow retrieve/intermediate' are all that are necessary to set someone on the right track. One never knows, but it could make a big difference for someone who is too shy or embarrassed to ask and should that happen we can rejoice with them in their good fortune. We have all been the beneficiary of helpful advice at some time and it is surely our duty to offer that same help to others.

One wonders whether those who are unwilling to assist think that if there are 10,000 trout in the water and a novice manages to catch a couple (if they are fortunate) the remaining 9,998 will be that much fewer to catch? You may perhaps consider that I am being overly harsh on those who wish to keep the source of their success to themselves, after all it is not a condition of buying a ticket, but I would suggest that the sport needs all the new blood it can muster in order to survive. It could well be that by discouraging novices, who subsequently give up due to a lack of initial success, fisheries will lose customers and therefore revenue and then be forced to close when there will be no fish for anyone to catch!

IMPACT OF *STILL WATER FLY-FISHING*

Into this scenario came Tom Ivens who, to the benefit of countless anglers worldwide and perhaps the ire of some of the more extreme Northampton school who wished that he had kept the results of their pioneering efforts within their closely guarded circle, decided to write his seminal book detailing how to tackle reservoirs and lakes with an artificial fly.

With the publication of *Still Water Fly-Fishing* Ivens' aim was *'to reveal as much as I know about the behaviour of trout in lakes and the methods of fly-fishing likely to be successful.'* For anglers who had little idea of where to start the book provided a comprehensive, step-by-step guide into the mysterious world of reservoir fly angling. Together with a couple of casting lessons it enabled fly anglers, both novice and experienced, to face the vast expanse of reservoir before them with a little less apprehension. Not surprisingly the book became an immediate bestseller.

Cyril Inwood (1911-1971)
Image courtesy of Bonhams

There is a story attached to all this (which may or may not be true). When it became known that Ivens was writing a book on the subject the Northampton group of fly fishers, headed largely by Cyril Inwood, being a secretive bunch closed ranks and Ivens was left very much on the periphery[6]. The story goes that one evening Ivens called at Inwood's house and, Inwood being out, his daughter proceeded to show Ivens the contents of her father's fly boxes which included his 'special' flies. When *Still Water Fly-Fishing* was published Inwood was furious, claiming that Ivens had stolen his ideas, and the two were never on close speaking terms again[7]. After that incident few ever saw the inside of Inwood's fly boxes again.

There may have been a bit of journalistic rivalry involved in all this. Tom Ivens was an accomplished author who had the ability to explain technical information with clarity, logic, enthusiasm and on occasion a little humour; and his book was a literary masterpiece in which he introduced a breadth of material that had not been seen in any angling work before. On the other hand, although Inwood was undoubtedly a brilliant angler, the task of writing a book of such complexity (with all the time-consuming research that it would have entailed) would probably have held little appeal to him. The truth of the matter will most likely never be fully known. Ivens, being an ex-naval officer was pretty straightforward in his dealings, as was Inwood, although the latter could be a bit dour at times. It was said that to be in the same boat as Inwood when you were a few fish in front was not a particularly memorable experience!

As I write this I have before me an article written by Cyril Inwood for *Trout & Salmon* magazine dated November 1960 entitled *Fly Fishing on Lakes and Reservoirs*. It is pretty rudimentary material and in it he gives nothing away of his flies and methods. It is curious to note that in the comprehensive list of *'my own choice of lures which I take with me each month through the season'* there are numerous traditional patterns, a brown and a green nymph are mentioned in passing, but there is no dressing given of any of the patterns that he would undoubtedly have used himself. Interestingly, there is no reference whatever to the Black & Peacock Spider.

It is pertinent to note that as a result of the publication of Ivens' book a great many of his flies are still well-known and treasured to this day whereas those that Inwood created (to the undoubted loss of the sport) died with him.

RESERVOIR TROUT FISHING CONTINUES TO ADVANCE

Reservoir fly fishing has continued to advance on every front in the seventy years that have passed since the publication of the first edition of *Still Water Fly-Fishing*. Nevertheless, despite the many changes, the fundamentals that Tom Ivens recommended of endeavouring to deceive the trout by adopting a 'thinking', scientific approach, employing deceivers rather than traditional patterns, are still very much as he advocated all those years ago.

Chapter 3

TRADITIONAL FLIES, DECEIVERS AND FLASHERS

As will shortly be seen, Tom Ivens had very firm ideas on the type of artificial fly necessary to tackle reservoir trout. It is therefore appropriate, before examining his patterns in detail, to consider his approach in some depth. His philosophy was very much bound up with the history of reservoir fly fishing in England which began with the construction of the first water supply reservoirs at the end of the nineteenth century and the beginning of the twentieth century to meet the demand for water from the big cities. Up until that time there were no large English lakes stocked with trout apart from those in the Lake District, although that part of the country was somewhat isolated until the construction of the railways. Before that time fly anglers who wished to fish large lakes generally travelled to Scotland to fish the lochs or to Ireland to fish the loughs.

The first reservoirs in England and Wales to be stocked with trout were Thrybergh Reservoir near Doncaster which was first

Loch Leven, Scotland

Public domain image

opened to trout anglers around 1880; Lake Vyrnwy, Powys in 1891; Ravensthorpe Reservoir, Northamptonshire in 1893; and Blagdon Lake, Somerset in 1904.

TRADITIONAL FLIES

When the new reservoirs were first opened to fly anglers it was only natural that they turned to the methods and flies that they had employed, with varying amounts of success, in Scotland, or if they had not fished Scotland themselves they would copy the methods from those who had. The standard technique was to use 'traditional' wet flies, retrieved quickly from a boat, to entice the trout into taking as a result of curiosity, annoyance, anger or territorial instinct. In order to be successful it required a stiff breeze to propel the boat and create a ripple to disguise the fly line and render the angler invisible. For obvious reasons the method was ineffective in conditions of flat calm. As far back as 1924, in *Loch-Fishing in Theory and Practice*, R C Bridgett had pointed out the limitations of the method and the need for a systematic approach using imitations of the trout's food. Although he recommended the use of nymphs, he somewhat bizarrely used traditional wet flies alongside them[8].

The traditional wet flies commonly employed were large, flashy and colourful and were very often based upon sea-trout and salmon flies. They were considerably larger than those used on rivers and many of them utilized double- and treble-hooks as well as spinning blades, fly spoons, beads, celluloid bodies and other adornments. Some were little more than spinners with a few strands of feather fibre attached and many were pretty formidable in appearance. In general there was little or no attempt to mimic the natural food of the trout in either its form or manner of movement.

EARLY ADVANCES BY DR BELL OF WRINGTON

That is how things stood until the emergence of Dr Bell of Wrington who began to fish Blagdon Lake in Somerset in 1920, shortly after his return from WW1. Dr Bell was a shy, reclusive but also very much a 'thinking' angler and he considered that, rather than use these gaudy flies to provoke the trout into taking, why not appeal to the fish's hunger by offering them something that resembles the food creatures they are ingesting every hour of the day.

Surely, Dr Bell reasoned, presenting an artificial fly that mimics a natural insect in shape, size and colour, and retrieving it in such a manner that it simulates the way in which a natural creature moves, must have a greater chance of success. After all, in order to grow and reproduce, stillwater trout spend most of their lives roaming the reservoir in search of food. The method worked on rivers and there was no reason to believe that it would not be equally successful on still water.

Rare image of Dr Bell of Wrington taken in 1945
Image courtesy of The Wrington Archive

As it was not possible to know for certain what creatures the trout are taking below the surface by observation, Dr Bell followed G E M Skues' example by spooning every fish he caught at Blagdon Lake and over the years he built up an extensive knowledge of all the organisms present. Once he had gained this information he set about the task of designing a series of fly patterns that would copy all the creatures he came across.

When Dr Bell tried his flies the results were truly astonishing. Despite the fact that they bore little resemblance to the traditional lake flies currently being used by everyone else, his flies caught fish and he very often came back with a limit bag when others had only a fish or two at most. What was also a new departure was that his patterns were successful at those times when the weather conditions were considered to be hopeless using traditional methods. He had proved beyond doubt that there were better and more consistent ways of taking reservoir trout.

Dr Bell made no attempt to publicize his work and, being a reclusive individual, all he wanted was to be left alone to fish Blagdon and so details of his flies are somewhat sketchy. This omission has recently been redressed with the publication of all the flies attributed to him and the full series, comprising thirty-five patterns, is documented in the author's book *Dr Bell's Trout Flies*.

BANK FISHING

It is appropriate at this point to highlight a highly significant divergence that was taking place from the traditional loch style methods commonly employed in Scotland. This was that the new developments in England were being made by anglers who were fishing primarily from the bank rather than from a boat.

One of the benefits of bank fishing was that it did not rely on having the stiff breeze necessary for the 'cast and lift' style to work and as a result it was possible to devise a range of alternative techniques to use depending on the prevailing weather conditions. It goes without saying that if the angler is able to have a method of fishing suitable for every circumstance likely to be encountered at his disposal it must increase the chances of *consistent* success.

It is relevant to note that both of the pioneers discussed in this chapter were bank fishers. Dr Bell was exclusively a bank angler (there is no record of him ever fishing from a boat) and Tom Ivens fished from a boat only infrequently.

TOM IVENS

The onset of WW2 temporarily halted the development of reservoir fly fishing but once hostilities ceased and life started to return to normal a new generation of fly anglers began to develop alternative techniques of tempting the trout. Among these innovators was a young man from Northampton named Tom Ivens.

When Ivens returned from military service at the end of WW2 he resumed his angling career at nearby Ravensthorpe Reservoir and Hollowell Reservoir. There he began to develop a new set of fly patterns, new methods of retrieving them and design a range of tackle specifically intended to present the flies at the long distances necessary on the vast expanses of still waters. His tackle innovations will be considered in a later chapter.

Ivens took the view that 'exact imitation' as it was currently being practised on the southern chalk streams[9] had little application to reservoirs. To his mind the influence of the chalk stream anglers led by such notable fly fishers as F M Halford[10] and G E M Skues[11] who were few in number, restricted to a tiny area of southern

Ravensthorpe Reservoir in Northamptonshire

England, and were socially elite, had too great an influence on the sport. The chalk stream purists[12] had taken the concept of 'exact imitation' to an unnecessarily complicated level by their insistance on copying down to the minutest detail everything about the creatures upon which the chalk stream trout fed. That would include size, shape, form, colour, translucency and perhaps even the sex of the natural creature.

Trout are voracious creatures, always on the lookout for food in order to grow, escape from predators and reproduce their kind; and to do this they need to feed continually and they simply do not have the time, intelligence or reasoning to inspect carefully every single creature they come across in order to determine whether or not it is a deception. To credit the fish with such a high level of intelligence, Ivens reasoned, was unrealistic and in any case is it really possible to produce an artificial fly that truly looks like the delicate form of a natural insect? Even if such a thing were feasible, could it be made to behave and progress in such a way that it would fool a trout – especially during a rise when the fish have dozens of examples around them to make a comparison? In Ivens' view that was not a valid option. The only logical alternative was to offer the fish something that does not replicate any single creature but nevertheless looks as though it might be food of some sort and so trigger the fish's instinctive feeding response.

Ivens went even further by proposing that it was very often the movement of the fly through the water, as much as the pattern itself, that provoked a positive reaction. Provided the fly was presented in such a manner that the fish was not alarmed it should achieve the desired effect on most occasions.

Tom Ivens with a 12½lb Border Esk salmon
Image courtesy of the Ivens family

DECEIVERS AND FLASHERS

Having settled upon the type of fly he considered necessary, Tom Ivens set about designing a small but comprehensive selection of flies to deal with all the circumstances that he was likely to face. These were attractor patterns which he divided into two distinct groups: 'deceivers' and 'flashers'. The deceivers were flies that the trout would take as representations of their natural food and needed to be recovered in a slow and lifelike manner and would form the first line of attack whenever the conditions were suitable. The flashers appealed to the fish by way of the shiny, tinsel materials employed in their construction or their bright colouration, or very often a combination of both. They were to be used whenever the wind and weather conditions were such that it was not possible to recover the flies delicately. It is these two groups of artificial flies that will be considered in the following chapters.

RIVER PATTERNS

At this point a few words about Tom Ivens' river patterns are no doubt appropriate. He adopted the same approach to rivers as he did to stillwaters by employing deceivers that were suggestions of the natural creatures rather than precise imitations. Once again he found that a small but comprehensive selection was sufficient to cover most of the situations that he was likely to encounter. Trout in moving water are, after all, exactly the same species as those in reservoirs and lakes; and those that have been stocked will very likely have been bred in the same hatchery.

There are five river patterns documented in this volume, three are his adaptations of traditional river flies that have been around for a great many years and two are specific creations intended solely for river work.

THE FUTURE OF FLY FISHING

Reservoir fly fishing has changed dramatically since those heady years of Blagdon, Hollowell, Ravensthorpe and Grafham as anglers and scientists have discovered more information about the behaviour of stillwater trout and the creatures upon which they feed. This has not unnaturally encouraged later generations of fly anglers, inspired by the logical and scientific methods introduced by Tom Ivens and his contemporaries, to develop further radical fly patterns and methods to deceive the trout. This continual progress must surely be a good and healthy development for the sport. The future for stillwater fly angling therefore looks encouraging!

Chapter 4

DISTANCE CASTING AND RETRIEVE METHODS

To state the obvious, bank fishing on reservoirs brings with it the necessity of presenting the flies where the fish are located and this entails fishing them at long range; and Tom Ivens was very much at the forefront in the development of long-distance fly casting techniques on stillwaters. The method involved double-haul casting in conjunction with a butt-action fly rod and double taper fly line for better and stealthier presentation. In essence it was an adaptation of tournament distance casting techniques that were modified for use in actual fishing conditions.

DOUBLE-HAUL CASTING

Double-haul casting involves keeping a tight line between the line hand and butt ring at all times apart from when line is being shot to extend line outside the tip ring on the forward and backward false casts and on the final delivery of the flies. In addition, line is hauled during the forward and backward rod movements in order to increase line speed and flex the rod, and so utilize its maximum power.

The distances that could be achieved were far in excess of those managed by river anglers, and the method needed time and practice to master, but it was possible to reach fish that were thirty yards away – and with great delicacy into the bargain.

The sequence was detailed in *Still Water Fly-Fishing* in a unique

Bank fishing at Eyebrook Reservoir

series of action photographs (drawings in the paperback edition) illustrating the technique and the method quickly became the accepted standard. Whilst it is true that there is nothing to beat one-to-one, qualified professional tuition, it probably remains the clearest illustration and explanation of fly casting committed to print.

Extracts from the double-haul casting sequence

© 2021 Adrian V W Freer

SHOOTING HEADS

The introduction of shooting heads (popularized by Geoffrey Bucknall in *Fly-Fishing Tactics on Still Water* in 1966) enabled anglers at Grafham and elsewhere to achieve even greater distances that were deemed necessary when fishing from the bank where, in general terms, the angler who was able to cast the furthest usually caught the most fish. Shooting heads became exceedingly popular for a while but they eventually went out of favour for normal work for a number of reasons. The weight of line being concentrated into a short length did not allow delicate presentation; snarling of the shooting line was a frequent occurrence (especially when nylon monofilament backing was used); and hooking trout at great distances was problematic due to the length of stretchy nylon between angler and fish. It is not a delicate method and it is as well to remember that in the early days of Grafham quickly retrieved lures were being used by the majority of anglers on relatively naive trout. Once the fish became more wary and difficult to catch it exposed the flaws of the system and more subtle and stealthy techniques became necessary.

WEIGHT FORWARD LINES

That advance came as anglers moved to weight-forward (or torpedo taper) plastic fly lines incorporating low- or non-stretch cores which were used in conjunction with fibre-glass and later carbon-fibre fly rods. The combination enabled anglers to cast as far as necessary but without any of the drawbacks that came with shooting heads. As a result reservoir angling became much easier, less tiring, more pleasurable and the greatest benefit of all was that hooking the fish at long range was far more consistent. Today the combination has become the accepted norm although a few trout anglers still use shooting heads for specific circumstances.

Shooting heads appear to be making something of a comeback amongst salmon anglers at the present time although whether this is a temporary or long-term development remains to be seen.

RECOVERY SPEEDS

One of the fundamentals of Ivens' approach, and something that was a significant departure at the time, was his insistence on retrieving his flies slowly or very slowly to make them appear lifelike. He considered it was of such importance that he went as far as to publish a table of recovery speeds for the various types of flies. These were documented as the length of time that was required to fish out an 18 yard cast, but as not all anglers cast and retrieve that distance every time his figures have been converted in the table below into seconds per foot which is probably easier for anglers to comprehend and make comparisons.

Fly Pattern	Speed	Retrieve	Seconds per Foot
All nymphs	Normal	Figure-of-eight	2.46
All nymphs	Slow	Figure-of-eight	2.96
Black & Peacock Spider	Normal	Figure-of-eight	1.63
Black & Peacock Spider	Slow	Figure-of-eight	1.89
Alexandra & Pretty Pretty	Normal	Figure-of-eight	1.15
Alexandra & Pretty Pretty	Fast	Figure-of-eight	0.81
Jersey Herd	Normal	Stripping	0.65
Jersey Herd	Fast	Stripping	0.52
Recovery Speeds Converted to Seconds per Foot			

© 2021 Adrian V W Freer

Looking at the recovery times in the table, although they were considered to be slow at a time when flies were normally fished either quickly or very quickly, they would perhaps be considered to be fairly fast by today's standards. Most present-day reservoir anglers (including the author) doubtless fish their nymph patterns considerably slower than the speeds in the above table and it is not uncommon to leave them stationary, recovering just sufficient line to keep in touch with the flies and no more. Writing in the 1970 edition of his book, Tom Ivens observed that when fishing the evening rise at Grafham, in order to avoid line wake his retrieve would take around four to five minutes.

It is interesting to note that Dr Bell, who was another angler who recovered his flies extremely slowly, once described the retrieve speed of his Amber Nymph, in the only article he wrote, like this: *'the draw in should be maddeningly slow, about two inches in a second.'* That equates to six seconds per foot.

Chapter 5

FLY DRESSING

Before moving on to examine the menus and fishing instructions for Tom Ivens' fly patterns it would perhaps be appropriate to digress for a moment to consider his approach to fly design and fly dressing.

Looking at his patterns, and bearing in mind how groundbreaking they were when they first appeared, there are several distinctive characteristics that immediately stand out. All his nymphs are straightforward in construction, are lightly dressed, use readily available materials, and are relatively drab in appearance mimicking the greens, olives, browns and blacks commonly encountered in sub-surface creatures. In contrast his flashers are all bright, flashy and colourful. His insistence on dressing the flies lightly was to produce artificials that were *'light and sparkling – never opaque – in silhouette.'* There are few difficult techniques involved and none of them will pose much of a problem for a fly tyer with only modest skills. Nevertheless, as simple as they are, the acid test for any fly is not whether it appeals to the human eye, requires great skill in tying or employs rare and expensive fur and plumage; but rather does it catch fish – and on that score all the flies pass this vital benchmark.

He used only natural herls, feathers, wool and hair for his patterns (although some were dyed) and during the intervening years synthetic materials have become increasingly popular and no doubt imaginative fly dressers could modify many of his patterns to improve them in some way. He also had a distinct partiality for hair wings, preferring them to those made from feather fibre due to their translucence and the way that they 'work' under the water.

NOTHING NEW UNDER THE SUN

When it comes to the design of 'new' fly patterns there is, of course, very little that is truly new under the sun. Nevertheless it has to be remarked that Tom Ivens' nymphs were quite unlike anything that had gone before. No doubt research would perhaps uncover a few obscure patterns that were invented a hundred years ago but a cursory glance at any fly catalogue of the period will show that they were very different from the run-of-the-mill flies of the time.

It is pertinent to note that two of the greatest twentieth century innovators of nymph patterns, Dr Bell and Frank Sawyer[13], both designed, it would appear independently of each other, a grub-type pattern (the Bell's Bug and Sawyer's Killer Bug) and Tom Ivens' Gentile is very much along the same sort of lines. Similarly, Ivens' Black Buzzer, introduced in 1970, bears an uncanny resemblance to Dr Bell's Blagdon Buzzer Nymph. Although the doctor made no attempt to publicize his work the dressing of this fly was published in an article written by Col Esmond Drury in the April 1956 issue of *Fishing Gazette*, and once Dr Bell's flies had been recognized as being successful Veal's of Bristol tied and sold copies of them commercially, and so it is possible that Ivens may have been familiar with the pattern.

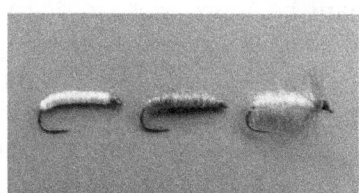

Bell's Bug (left), Sawyer's Killer Bug (centre) and Ivens' Gentile (right)

There is, of course, nothing amiss with copying and modifying flies devised by others and that is the way that fly design has very often progressed down the years.

Dr Bell's Blagdon Buzzer Nymph (left) and T C Ivens' Black Buzzer (right)

TRIGGER POINTS

One conspicuous feature that recurs in Tom Ivens' fly patterns is the incorporation of a prominent head of wound peacock herl which was intended to provide a target point for the fish to home in on. All four nymphs and the Jersey Herd from his first series of flies incorporate this feature, as does the Buzzer and Daddy Long Legs from his second series, as well as the March Brown and Green Nymph (River Version) from his river flies.

I have for many years sought to incorporate a bold head in many of my own patterns, coated with at least two layers of shiny varnish, which I consider provides a definite aiming point for the fish to concentrate on and I am convinced that it does make a material difference (and improvement). Being the forward-thinking angler that he was there seems little doubt that Tom Ivens thought along much the same lines many years before I did.

DRESSING MENUS

In the fly menus that follow, the hook sizes that Tom Ivens recommended have been detailed and, as is my usual practice when listing fly dressings, the configuration of the hackle is indicated in every case as very often this can make a material difference to the appearance of the fly and, just as importantly, its manner of progression through the water.

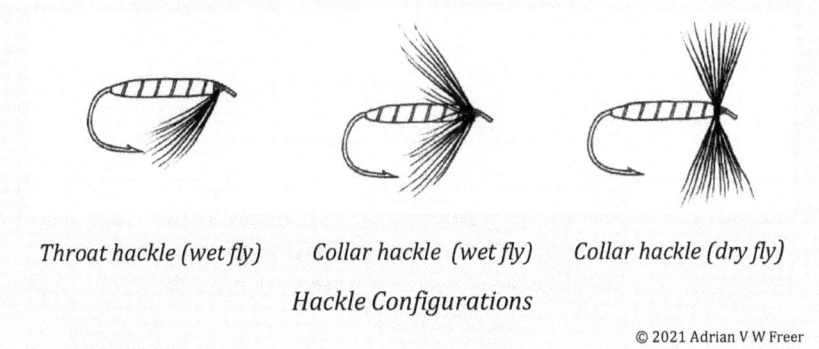

Throat hackle (wet fly)   Collar hackle (wet fly)   Collar hackle (dry fly)

Hackle Configurations

© 2021 Adrian V W Freer

HOOK SCALES AND SIZES

For the avoidance of confusion a few words about the hook scales and hook sizes used in this book are probably appropriate. New Scale (Pennell) hooks sizes (which are obsolete today) were used in the first two editions of *Still Water Fly-Fishing* and Old Scale (Redditch) hook sizes (currently in use today) were used in the third and fourth editions. In this present volume the Old Scale (Redditch) has been used throughout.

On a practical note, in several instances Tom Ivens specified odd numbered hook sizes which are no longer available and rather than arbitrarily attempt to round them up or down they have been left as Ivens suggested and it is up to each fly dresser to choose the sizes they consider to be the most appropriate for their requirements. A conversion table of the two hook scales is appended below for those with the first two editions of his book.

Old Scale (Redditch)	New Scale (Pennell)
2	
4	
6	9
8	7
10	5
12	3
14	1
16	00
18	

Conversion Table of Hook Sizes

© 2021 Adrian V W Freer

Although the patterns in the following chapters have been around for a good many years, and like many other flies of the period many of them have been superseded in favour of newer (but not necessarily better) creations, they are all flies that have stood the test of time and are still worth a try!

Chapter 6

T C IVENS' ORIGINAL (1952) SERIES OF FLY PATTERNS

Tom Ivens' original (1952) series of flies, described in *Still Water Fly-Fishing*, are undoubtedly some of the best known and widely used reservoir patterns of all time. There are five deceiver nymphs which need to be recovered slowly for best effect and should form the first line of attack, and three flashers for which a fast recovery is necessary. There is also a dry fly should the angler decide to fish dry. Together they form a comprehensive set that should cope with pretty well every eventuality a reservoir fly angler is likely to face.

The intention was that the nymphs should be dissimilar in profile, providing variety, but conform to the premise that they suggest food creatures that the trout would recognize and take with confidence. The flashers display distinct variations in size, shape and colour. Their effectiveness can be judged by the fact that many are still in common usage and listed in present-day fly catalogues.

We are informed that the flies in this chapter were responsible for ninety-six per cent of Tom Ivens' total catch between 1947 and 1952 and that just four of them accounted for eighty-five per cent of the total. Somewhat infuriatingly though, we are not told which of the flies make up that select four! It takes a great deal of courage to restrict fly choice to such a tiny number but Tom Ivens had every faith in them. Whether used for rainbows or browns they are flies that can be selected and fished with confidence today.

Evening fishing at Hollowell Reservoir, c.1950s
Image courtesy of the Ivens family

Brown & Green Nymph   *Brown Nymph*
Black & Peacock Spider
Green & Yellow Nymph   *Green Nymph*
Jersey Herd
Alexandra   *Pretty Pretty*
Flies from T C Ivens' Original (1952) Series of Flies
Flies supplied by Benwoods of London, c.1965

Black & Peacock Spider

Hook: Wet fly hook sizes 6 – 12
Most useful sizes: 8 – 9
Tying thread: Black
Body: Bronze peacock herl over floss underbody, ribbed with tying thread for strength
Hackle: Long-fibred black hen collar hackle
Head: Tying thread, clear varnished
Variants: Tandem and streamer versions can be tied, see the comments below.

This pattern is inextricably linked with the name of Tom Ivens and it must surely be his most well-known, popular and successful fly and many novices have used it in their first attempt at fly dressing. Although he undoubtedly popularized the fly in all probability it has its roots long before the first reservoirs were even thought of[14].

In his book he makes the comment that at one stage he would have cheerfully gone out with just this one fly, in a range of sizes, but it did let him down on occasion whereupon he was obliged to come up with a few alternatives. There is an interesting account of how the fly came into being. Tom had been fishing, without success, using an Alder pattern and looking at it he considered it to be too heavily dressed and so he cut off the wings and carried on fishing.

After this drastic alteration the fly began to work and with just a few minor changes (in all probability the substitution of a longer hackle and the body being plumped up by the addition of the floss underbody) the fly was subsequently renamed the Black & Peacock Spider and the rest is history.

It is a fly that needs to be fished slowly at all times and it can represent pretty much any creature present in reservoirs. It can be used to tackle fish that are taking nymphs just subsurface, when the trout are chasing sticklebacks and fish fry, during the silverhorns rise, and deep down in the larger sizes.

Tandem Black & Peacock Spider

There are occasions when the trout are located deep down and a very large fly is necessary to gain their attention. At such times a size 8 or 10 tandem version of the Black & Peacock, fished from a boat, is possibly one of the best options. As a further variation, the addition of a wing of black-dyed polar bear hair mixed with a few strands of peacock herl transforms the B&P into a streamer.

The distinctive contrast and outline of large flies such as this enable them to stand out at depth when smaller patterns would be overlooked, and they are likely to account for some of the larger specimens that rarely come to a single fly (black is a colour that stands out well in the depths and in coloured water).

Green Nymph

Hook: Wet fly hook sizes 7 – 12
Most useful sizes: 9 – 10
Tying thread: Black
Body: Tapered white floss underbody, over-wrapped with green-dyed nylon monofilament
Hackle: Brown partridge collar hackle
Head: Peacock herl twisted and wound to form a bold head
Variant: The hackle can be omitted in very small sizes. A version of this fly specifically designed for rivers is described in chapter ten.

There are occasions when there is little activity to be seen and no breeze to blow terrestrial creatures on to the surface. At such times the fish may well be feeding, but right on the reservoir bed on a variety of larvae, nymphs and water bugs.

This is a heavy fly intended to get down to the bottom quickly where it needs to be recovered slowly with a series of six inch pulls and pauses. The trout will often be feeding confidently and a take may manifest itself as a slow draw or else a firm pull as the fish feels the hook point and bolts in alarm. Be prepared for a smash take that may well catch you by surprise. Subsurface fishing demands concentration and it often seems that just when your mind begins to wander, that is the instant when a fish decides to take.

Brown Nymph

Hook: Wet fly hook sizes 7 – 12
Most useful sizes: 9 – 10
Tying thread: Black
Back: Two strands of stripped, green-dyed ostrich herl
Body: Brown-dyed ostrich herl, ribbed with oval gold tinsel
Horns: Two strands of peacock herl
Head: Peacock herl twisted and wound to form a bold head
Variants: This pattern can be simplified in the smaller sizes by omitting the ostrich herl back and substituting dubbed brown wool for the body.

This is a lighter fly than the Green Nymph and it therefore fishes higher in the water column. When the fish are moving in the top few feet of water, or taking nymphs ascending to the surface to hatch, this is a very suitable pattern to employ. It is particularly useful for those occasions when olive nymphs are the source of the trout's attention.

    Cast the fly out and let it sink, varying the countdown each time until you get an offer, and once you have located the fish repeat the same interval every time. It is a fly that needs a slow figure-of-eight recovery to complete the deception and wait for some decisive takes.

Green & Yellow Nymph

Hook: Wet fly hook sizes 10 – 12
Most useful sizes: 11 – 12
Tying thread: Black
Body: Rear half of body green-dyed swan herl, front half of body deep yellow-dyed swan herl
Head: Peacock herl twisted and wound to form a bold head

This is a light, sparsely dressed fly that was designed to fish high in the water for those occasions when the trout are feeding at or just beneath the surface. It is very likely that at such times they are taking buzzer pupae, either as they rise and fall within the top few inches of water prior to hatching, or alternatively when they are at the point of emergence, resting stationary within the surface film. There is little doubt that buzzers (chironomids) form the greatest proportion of the diet of lowland reservoir trout.

When fishing this fly, little or no movement is necessary and all that is required is to keep a tight line to remain in touch, with the breeze or current providing all the action that is necessary. When trout are feeding on buzzer pupae they generally take quite confidently and decisive pulls can be expected, with the fish very often hooking themselves in the process. Despite its unassuming profile this is nonetheless a very killing pattern.

Brown & Green Nymph

Hook: Wet fly hook sizes 6 – 10
Tying thread: Black
Tail: Peacock herl
Body: Green-dyed and brown-dyed ostrich herl wound together to form a segmented body, ribbed with oval gold tinsel
Back: Peacock herl
Head: Peacock herl twisted and wound to form a bold head
Variant: Tie with a leaded underbody.

Tom Ivens was of the opinion that there are occasions when the trout collectively seem to lose interest in a particular make of fly and a change of pattern can rekindle their attention (third edition, pages 181/182). This fly was designed for such times as an alternative to the Green Nymph and Brown Nymph.

It is somewhat 'fish-shaped' in silhouette and it can be employed to tackle trout that are gorging on small fry. Alternatively it can be fished downwind from a boat, five feet or so down, recovering line fairly quickly when the fish will frequently take with a firm pull.

Its outline and colouration make it a good general prospecting pattern to try when nothing is showing and you do not know quite where to start. This is probably one of the most widely used of Tom Ivens' nymphs today and it is still listed in many fly catalogues.

Pretty Pretty

Hook: Wet fly hook sizes 6 – 9
Most useful size: 7
Tying thread: Black
Tag: Silver tinsel
Tail: Golden pheasant topping feather
Body: Floss underbody, over-wrapped with peacock herl and green-dyed ostrich herl twisted together, ribbed with oval silver tinsel
Hackle: Green-dyed hen collar hackle, two turns
Wing: Goat hair dyed orange-yellow
Head: Tying thread, clear varnished

Tom Ivens' first series of flies included three flasher patterns that were designed to be fished fast. The first of them, the Pretty Pretty, is fairly conventional in construction and it looks appealing to both angler and (presumably) the fish. Having said that, it is a fly that seems to have gone out of favour nowadays and I do not know of any angler who currently carries one.

When dressing the fly it is essential not to incorporate too much goat hair in order for it to sink rapidly and subsequently not rise to the surface when being retrieved quickly. Experience over a number of seasons proved conclusively that it was much more effective with rainbows than with browns.

Jersey Herd

Hook: Long shank lure hook size 6
Tying thread: Black
Tail: Twelve strands of peacock herl
Body: Floss underbody tied to a fish profile, over-wrapped with copper coloured tinsel
Back: Peacock herl
Hackle: Short-fibred rich orange cock collar hackle (doubled), two turns
Head: Peacock herl twisted and wound to form a bold head
Variant: It may be tied with a leaded underbody.

This fly was designed to produce a heavy fly that would stay beneath the surface when stripped through very quickly in blustery wind conditions when lighter flies came to the surface. It also makes an excellent fry imitation for use when the fish are sticklebacking from late-summer onwards. The somewhat unusual name derives from the fact that the foil cap from a Jersey milk bottle was used in the prototype fly.

The dressing of this fly has probably suffered more abuse at the hand of errant fly tyers than any other (very often gold tinsel is used instead of copper, the tapered floss underbody is omitted, and a yellow hackle is substituted) but this is the original dressing.

Alexandra

Hook: Wet fly hook sizes 6 – 11 (but see the comment below†)
Tying thread: Black
Tail: Red ibis (substitute)
Body: Silver tinsel, over-ribbed with oval silver tinsel
Hackle: Black hen throat hackle
Wing: Green peacock sword tail fibres
Topping: Golden x Amherst topping feather
Head: Tying thread, clear varnished

Among his original series of flies the Alexandra is the only 'standard' pattern which appears and it is very similar to the traditional version with the single but essential difference that it is much more lightly dressed than most commercially tied flies.

The usage of flashers is confined to those occasions when the wind is such that it is impossible to keep in touch with slowly recovered nymphs and it is necessary to use a fly that is retrieved fast or very fast; with bright colours and flash to complete the deception.

†The comment is made that in conditions of bright sunshine, very small sizes of this pattern, 15s and 16s, fished slowly near the surface can induce takes but nevertheless bring with them the problem of holding the fish on such small hooks.

Fuzzy Buzzy

Hook: Dry fly hook sizes 7 – 12
Tying thread: Black
Body: Oval gold tinsel
Hackles: Two stiff, brown cock hackles wound as a dry fly collar hackle at the bend of the hook, and two stiff, brown cock hackles wound as a dry fly collar hackle at the head, they may be clipped short for better floatation
Head: Tying thread, clear varnished
Variants: The hackle colours may be varied as desired and contrasting colours can be employed to give a 'bi-visible' fly.

Although it may not always be a productive method, dry fly fishing must surely rank as one of the most exciting and this was Ivens' pattern for use at such times. There are few experiences that surpass that sublime moment when your fly is sitting on the surface and the snout of a trout breaks through, engulfs the fly, turns down, and you tighten into a hard-fighting fish. It can also be employed as a 'wake fly', slowly drawn along the surface as twilight approaches.

Since the earlier editions of *Still Water Fly-Fishing* were written rainbows have increasingly replaced browns and dry fly fishing has become an increasingly popular, and more to the point, an increasingly successful tactic.

Chapter 7

RAVENSTHORPE RESERVOIR AND HOLLOWELL RESERVOIR

Tom Ivens did much of his experimental work at two reservoirs close to his home: Ravensthorpe Reservoir and Hollowell Reservoir. They are situated side-by-side ten miles north of Northampton and just to the west of the A5199. There he spent many hours perfecting his flies, tackle and fishing techniques, and also enjoyed many enjoyable fishing forays into the bargain – after all fishing should always be fun!

RAVENSTHORPE RESERVOIR

The history of Ravensthorpe Reservoir dates back to Victorian times and it was first opened as a trout fishery in 1893. It is a beautiful and well-matured water that covers an area of 100 acres (of which 90 acres are fishable) with a maximum depth of 30 feet when full. In the early years it was mainly stocked with browns (a few rainbows were introduced in 1952 and 1953) although like most trout

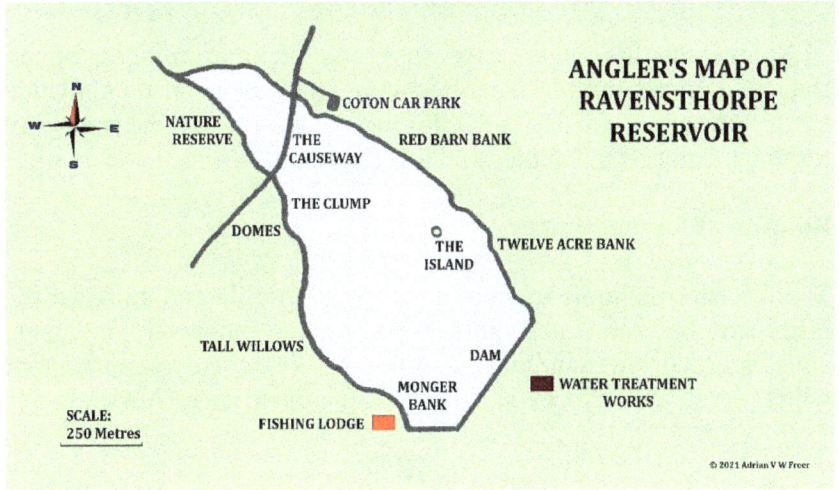

fisheries nowadays rainbows predominate. It boasts a history of some phenomenal catches: in 1895 the season's average weight was 3lb 5½oz and in 1896 Rev Charles Brooke had an eight-fish limit that weighed 38lb 12oz (average: 4lb 13½oz).

It is currently operated very much as a 'big fish' water and the records currently stand at 17lb 15oz for rainbow trout, 10lb for brown trout and 44lb 12oz for pike.

Ravensthorpe Reservoir

Natural fly life there is profuse and includes midges, olives, sedges, damsels and corixae. Recommended artificial flies include Black Buzzers, Damsels, Gold Ribbed Hare's Ears, Pheasant Tail Nymphs, Emergers, Daddies and lures.

Wildlife at Ravensthorpe

The reservoir is home to an abundance of wildlife and amongst the birds to be seen are goldeneye, smew, shoveler, widgeon, goosander, curlew, sandpiper and hobby; with the occasional great white egret and osprey putting in an appearance. Amongst the mammals present are otters, badgers, red foxes and muntjac deer as well as seven species of bat.

HOLLOWELL RESERVOIR

Hollowell Reservoir, which Tom Ivens also fished, is considerably newer and it was first opened as a water supply reservoir in 1938. It extends to an area of 140 acres with a maximum depth of 32 feet when full.

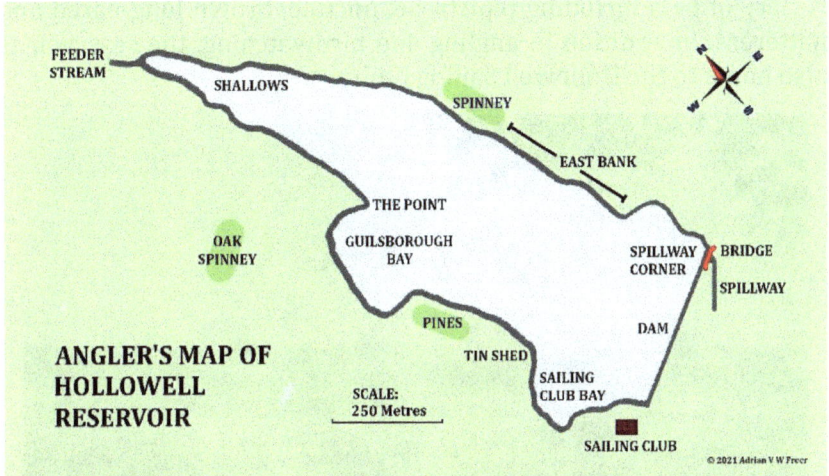

When construction was complete it was stocked with brown trout (rainbows have never been stocked at Hollowell) and during that time it produced large fish on a regular basis. In *The Art of Angling* Tom Ivens recorded that in 1948 he had witnessed the capture of a brown trout weighing 5½lb. Hollowell continued as a fly fishery for a number of years but from 1955 onwards it began to suffer serious problems with a build-up in the pike and perch populations which eventually destroyed it as a trout water and it subsequently closed to trout fishing in 1958.

Since that time it has operated as a coarse fishery holding good stocks of specimen carp, pike, tench, bream, roach and perch, and there is also a large head of roach x bream hybrids. It is by all accounts not an easy water to fish but it does yield quality fish (many tench in excess of 10lb have been recorded) to anglers who are prepared to put in the time and effort.

Wildlife at Hollowell

The reservoir and its surrounding area are host to a variety of wildlife: the birds including grey phalaropes, dunlins, ringed plovers, wheatear, rock pipits, hobbies and ospreys. Amongst the larger mammals to be seen are badgers, otters, weasels and a wide variety of bats including pipistrelle, noctule, brown long-eared and natterers. In addition to angling and birdwatching, the reservoir is also home to the Hollowell Sailing Club.

Hollowell Reservoir

Just as in the 1920s and 1930s when many of the early developments in reservoir fly fishing took place at Blagdon, these two Northamptonshire reservoirs were the setting for the revolutionary advances of the 1950s and 1960s. Although they have been somewhat overshadowed in later years with the opening of the three big Anglian Water reservoirs, Pitsford, Grafham and Rutland, they nonetheless still occupy a unique position in the annals of angling history.

Chapter 8

T C IVENS' SECOND (1970/75) SERIES OF FLY PATTERNS

The primary intention behind the design of Tom Ivens' second series of flies was to provide him with a few alternative patterns to deal with situations that were unique to Grafham Water which he fished from July 1966 onwards. Seven new flies were introduced in the 1970 edition of *Still Water Fly-Fishing* with a further three in the 1975 edition. It is important to emphasize that they were intended to complement rather than replace those of his original (1952) series which still formed the first line of attack.

When it first opened in 1966, Grafham was totally unlike any reservoir available to English fly fishers. It was by far the largest in the country, it was much deeper which allowed for stratification, there was an abundance of bottom feed which gave rise to phenomenal growth rates in the early years and the stock of trout, both browns and rainbows, were vigorous feeders willing to chase a fly and take the angler down to the backing (if not the horizon) on their first run. Whilst these patterns may not be quite as well-known as his original set, they are still very useful flies well worth giving a try.

On a practical fly dressing note, in this chapter there are several instances where Tom Ivens did not document the recommended hook sizes or dressing materials. Where this is the case the author has suggested appropriate sizes and materials which it is hoped will prove helpful and they are identified in the menus with an asterisk*.

Bank fishing in Pig's Bay, Grafham Water
Image courtesy of Colin Brett

The Fly Fishing Legacy of T C Ivens

Black Buzzer   *Claret Buzzer*   *Green Buzzer*

Black Knight   *Gentile*   *Cinnamon & Gold*

Hair Wing Butcher   *Polar Bear*

Daddy Long Legs

Black Knight Tandem Streamer

Whisky Fly   *Muddler Minnow*   *Sticky Willy*

T C Ivens' Second (1970/75) Series of Flies

Gentile

Hook: Wet fly hook sizes 11 – 16
Tying thread: Black
Body: Dubbed mixture of white and yellow chopped wool, tied to a maggot shape, slender at the bend and thickening towards the head
Hackle: Ginger hen collar hackle, clipped short
Head: Tying thread, clear varnished

Tom Ivens described this fly as resembling something between a caddis grub and a bluebottle maggot. There is probably a play on words with the name – the somewhat old-fashioned term for maggots was gentles and in colouration it is not dissimilar to the coarse angler's bait. The rationale behind its construction is however a little hard to fathom because we do not see caddis larvae outside their cases and reservoir fly anglers do not fish with maggots. Nevertheless it does give the impression of being something edible and tasty to the fish.

This pattern was recommended for rainbows at those times when they are feeding at the surface on small and unidentifiable 'bugs' of some sort when it should be fished extremely slowly. It proved to be very successful during bright, sunny conditions and also at dusk. Flies such as this may not inspire much confidence due to their simplicity but that is no bar to success.

Buzzer

Hook: Wet fly hook sizes 9 – 10
Tying thread: Black
Body: Black, claret or emerald-green wool tied part way round the bend, ribbed with fine silver wire
Thorax: Black, claret or emerald-green wool to match the body
Wing: Short tuft of white wool, hair or feather fibre
Head: Peacock herl twisted and wound to form a bold head
Variants: The colour of the wool and rib can be permutated endlessly to match the natural on the water and no doubt smaller hook sizes to those recommended would prove to be just as, or even more, successful.

Once the supreme importance of buzzer pupae in the diet of reservoir trout became known everyone seemed to come up with their own version, although why it took quite so long is anyone's guess. As has already been remarked this fly bears a close resemblance to Dr Bell's pattern which came more than a generation earlier.

In the fishing instructions, Tom Ivens suggested that it produces the best results when it is fished two feet to six feet down, drawn very slowly to avoid any suggestion of line wake; with the alternative tactic of recovering a foot of line at a time and leaving a long pause between each pull. Whatever method is chosen it is agreed that takes can be very firm.

Current thinking would suggest that when buzzers are being taken at the surface the flies should either be left static or alternatively retrieved extremely slowly to allow them to rise and fall very gently just a few inches beneath the surface film. It goes to demonstrate that at the time of the opening of Grafham Water, when the fly was first developed, buzzer fishing was still very much in its infancy.

There is no mention by Ivens of the use of 'emergers' which we now know can be an absolutely deadly tactic when employed on the appropriate occasion.

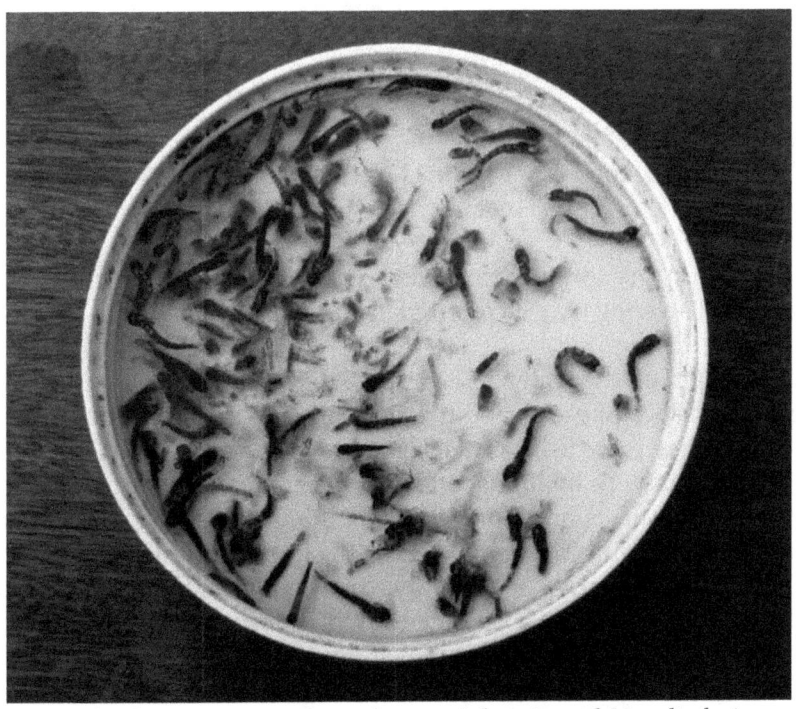

Result of an autopsy performed on a rainbow in mid-May disclosing dozens of black buzzer pupae

Cinnamon & Gold

Hook: Wet fly hook sizes 9 – 15
Tying thread: Black
Body: Oval or flat gold tinsel
Hackle: Ginger cock collar hackle (doubled), two turns
Wing: Bunch of ginger cock hackle fibres or cinnamon partridge wing
Head: Tying thread, clear varnished
Variant: The wing may be omitted in sizes 13 and smaller.

When Grafham first opened it became necessary to come up with a few alternative patterns and this derivative of the Wickham's Fancy was intended to be used as a deceiver despite its tinsel body.

It was found to be highly effective fished near the surface from a boat in calm lanes and during a flat calm, and in the smaller sizes during the evening rise recovered with short, quick draws with the rod point held high as a 'wake fly' that lightly furrows the surface. The belly in the line between the rod tip and water allows the fish to turn down before tightening which gives a greater opportunity of hooking the fish.

It is a versatile fly that can be employed in a wide range of situations and proved successful in the larger sizes for browns, recovered with a medium-fast retrieve, in coloured water.

Polar Bear

Hook: Long shank lure hook sizes 4 – 8, or standard size 6
Tying thread: White
Body: White fur, hair, wool or chenille, ribbed with flat silver tinsel
Wing: White polar bear hair (alternatively use white swan herl or ram's wool)
Head: Tying thread, clear varnished
Variant: It may also be tied with two hooks in tandem.

During the early months following the opening of Grafham Water the Missionary (a fly that originates from New Zealand) and variations of it were responsible for much of the carnage. The Polar Bear is one such derivative.

This is a very easily-constructed fly that does well when fished deep down and quite slowly. It is also good when stripped through the water very fast close to the surface. As with the Pretty Pretty, it is essential not to incorporate too much hair in the wing or it will tend to surface as a result.

When the fly is wet, the body takes on an attractive, translucent appearance with the semi-transparency and flash making it an excellent representation of a small fish. Give it a try when the trout are harrowing fry in the margins which occurs from late-summer onwards.

Black Knight

Hook: Wet fly hook sizes 6 – 12*
Tying thread: Black
Body: Oval gold or oval silver tinsel, alternatively flat tinsel over-ribbed with oval tinsel for extra flash
Hackle: Black hen collar hackle, three turns
Head: Tying thread, clear varnished
Variant: See the tandem version later in this chapter.

In both its single- and double-hook versions the Black Knight is typical of the sort of flasher pattern that was popular in the early years of Grafham to tackle its energetic rainbows which liked nothing more than to chase a swiftly moving fly. Although it is quite uncomplicated in its construction it possesses brightness and movement which renders it a good representation of the tiny fry that are abundant in all reservoirs.

Once fly dressers progress beyond the novice stage there is always the very real temptation to add a few extra 'refinements' to make flies like this more attractive, but which in reality are no improvement and can actually be counterproductive. Perhaps following Tom Ivens' advice by tying two sets of flies, one designed to appeal to the trout and another to show off the fly dresser's skill, is not a bad idea after all.

Hair Wing Butcher

Hook: Wet fly hook sizes 6 – 12*
Tying thread: Black
Tail: Red ibis (substitute)
Body: Flat silver tinsel, over-ribbed with oval silver tinsel
Hackle: Black hen throat hackle
Wing: Black squirrel hair, tied to lie low over the body like a streamer wing
Head: Tying thread, clear varnished
Variant: Also recommended was the traditional feather-winged Butcher with a wing of blue/black mallard feather.

Somewhat surprisingly, although he had dismissed traditional wet flies many years previously (with the single exception of the Alexandra), Tom Ivens returned to the Butcher which he fished medium-fast towards dusk to tackle the fast-growing trout at Grafham. For reasons that are still not fully understood these Grafham trout were exceptionally fast-growing, vigorous fish that enjoyed pursuing flies that were bright, colourful and flashy.

Tom Ivens recreated his version incorporating an over-rib of oval silver tinsel to increase the flash, and a hair wing in place of the customary feather which he considered to be much more appealing and had greater translucency and inbuilt action.

Daddy Long Legs (or Crane Fly)

Hook: Dry fly hook size 10*
Tying thread: Dark brown*
Body: Dark brown tying thread*
Legs: Six cock pheasant centre tail fibres, each knotted once and tied at 60, 90 and 120 degrees to the hook shank, three on either side*
Wing: Two brown cock hackles, one tied each side at 120 degrees to the hook shank*
Head/thorax: Peacock herl*
Variant: When used in conjunction with a conventional fly line a brown cock dry fly collar hackle* may be necessary to aid floatation.

This fly is illustrated in the colour plate of the second series of patterns in *Still Water Fly-Fishing* where it is discussed in conjunction with dapping, although the dressing is not given.

As autumn approaches daddy long legs (in a good year for them) are very often blown on to the water and the angler who has the right pattern can have a bumper time. Despite Ivens' assertion that exact imitations are a waste of time this is a really close copy. When trout are observed to be taking daddies, position yourself where the naturals are being blown on to the water and cast the fly into the general area of activity – and expect some explosive takes!

Black Knight Tandem Streamer

Hooks: Two size 8 or 10 wet fly hooks tied in tandem
Tying thread: Black
Front body: Oval gold or oval silver tinsel, alternatively flat tinsel over-ribbed with oval tinsel for extra flash
Front hackle: Black hen collar hackle, three turns
Wing: Black-dyed polar bear hair mixed with a few strands of peacock herl
Front head: Tying thread, clear varnished
Rear body: Oval gold or oval silver tinsel, alternatively flat tinsel over-ribbed with oval tinsel for extra flash
Rear hackle: Black hen collar hackle, three turns
Rear head: Tying thread, clear varnished
Variants: Tom Ivens' other flasher patterns can all be tied either in tandem format or as a tandem streamer as required.

On those occasions when the fish are lying deep down, for example on hot, bright and still days, large flies such as this are very suitable for use from a boat in conjunction with a sinking line employing a slow or medium retrieve.

When endeavouring to tempt one of those monsters of the deep that are not interested in small fare but live on a fish diet, try this fly, fished quite slowly.

Whisky Fly (or Whiskey Fly)

Hook: Long shank lure hook sizes 6 – 9
Tying thread: Orange
Tag: Red fluorescent floss or wool
Body: Oval gold tinsel
Hackle: Hot orange-dyed calf tail, polar bear hair or coarse wool
Wing: Hot orange-dyed calf tail, polar bear hair or coarse wool
Head: Red fluorescent floss or wool, clear varnished; or red varnish
Variants: Tom Ivens used four different versions of this fly, all of which appeared to kill equally well.

The final three flies in this chapter were first described in the 1975 edition of *Still Water Fly-Fishing*.

The Whisky Fly proved to be an excellent killer of rainbows at Grafham, fished medium-fast to fast, with the recovered line dropped into a line-raft, line-tray or the bottom of the boat. As a result of its phenomenal success it became one of Tom Ivens' 'standard' patterns to use in the early part of the season; with 'white' flies (such as the Polar Bear, Gentile and Sticky Willy) being his preferred choice from mid-June onwards.

Somewhat surprisingly, in view of his outstanding catches of rainbows with this pattern, Tom Ivens could not recall catching a brown trout using it.

Muddler Minnow

Hook: Long shank hook sizes 6 – 9
Tying thread: Black
Tail: Brown turkey
Body: Oval gold tinsel
Wing: Brown turkey
Head: Spun natural deer hair trimmed to form a bold, ball-shaped head with a few fibres left above and below the hook shank pointing towards the rear as a throat hackle and an over-wing
Variant: The Whisky Muddler, based on the previous pattern, substitutes hot orange-dyed hair for the tail and wing.

Uses of the Muddler Minnow are endless: it can be fished on a sunk line close to the bottom using either a slow draw or a draw-and-pause recovery, stripped through quickly, trolled, or side-cast from a drifting boat. It can also be also used as a 'popping bug'.

When the rules at Grafham were revised to permit trolling and side-casting from a rowed boat, it opened up a valuable new tactic to try when other techniques were proving ineffective. The Muddler Minnow and Whisky Muddler were two of the most popular and successful flies to use with the method. The importance of trolling was such that Tom Ivens deemed it necessary to add a new chapter describing the technique to the 1975 edition of his book.

Sticky Willy

Hook: Wet fly or long shank hook sizes 6 – 12*
Tying thread: None
Body: Assorted mixture of white hair, wool, feather or fur cut into $3/16$ inch to $1/2$ inch lengths and blended together, glued to the hook shank with Evo-Stik or Araldite, allowed to dry and then finally clipped to a maggot shape
Head: None

In the 1970s white flies such as Tom Ivens' Polar Bear and Gentile, as well as the Rasputin and Baby Doll, were all proving extremely popular and successful at Grafham. This rather strange pattern was designed to produce another white fly, but this time with the body made up of a mixture of different (white) materials to present a translucent, iridescent effect in order to attract the fish.

The reason for making the fly with adhesive rather than using tying thread was simply that Ivens considered dubbing the body to be a rather laborious process (I must confess that I rather enjoy performing the procedure). Minimal flies like this can undoubtedly be turned out at a rapid rate although I would question whether that alone is sufficient justification for employing the technique. For some reason white flies seem to be somewhat less popular at the present time.

Chapter 9

GRAFHAM WATER

When Grafham Water first opened to trout fishing in 1966 it was the largest and deepest man-made body of water in England with a surface area of 1,550 acres and a depth of 69 feet when full[15]. Grafham was instrumental in what has been described as the 'stillwater revolution' when many thousands of anglers turned to fly fishing for the first time. Prior to its opening Grafham was stocked with 15,000 brown and 53,000 rainbow trout and the phenomenal growth rates, fighting qualities and size of the fish at that time remain unsurpassed to this day.

Grafham possesses an abundance of aquatic and fly life: buzzers, sedges, daphnia, damsels, snails and latterly the infamous killer shrimp, all of which provide food for the trout and fly fishing of exceptional quality with grown-on, specimen fish caught every year.

Recommended flies include Buzzers, Diawl Bachs, Daddies and Minkies. The current records stand at rainbow trout 13lb 13oz (1992), brown trout 17lb 2oz (1994; a bait-caught brownie

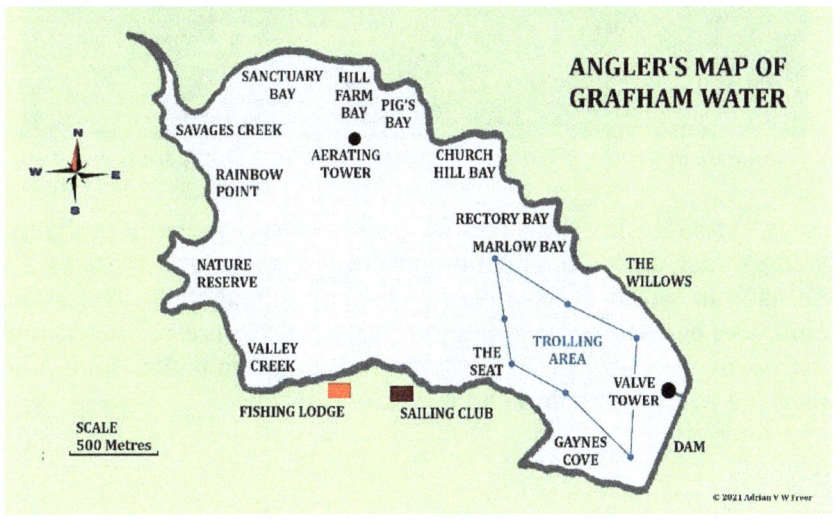

weighing 19lb 12oz was landed in 1996), pike 34lb 8oz (2014) and a zander of 22lb (2010) which currently holds the UK record.

Trolling under oar power became a permitted method at Grafham as a result of a rule change in 1972 (see map).

Wildlife at Grafham

The reservoir is set within a 1,992 acre Site of Special Scientific Interest (SSSI) and is host to a diverse assortment of wildlife. Birds to be seen include nuthatches, tree creepers, greater spotted woodpeckers and nightingales; water birds including mallards,

Sunrise at Grafham Water, taken from 'The Seat' on the south bank
Image courtesy of Bob Meadows

coots, tufted ducks, great crested grebes and great northern divers; waders such as common sandpipers and dunlins; and more rarely perhaps an osprey or Slavonian grebe. The animal life is diverse and embraces everything from muntjac deer to great crested newts and warty newts; and invertebrates including common blue and marbled white butterflies and even glow worms.

Chapter 10

T C IVENS' RIVER PATTERNS

As has already been noted, Tom Ivens also had a keen interest in river trout fishing and, just as on reservoirs, he found that a small number of patterns was sufficient to deal with all the situations he was likely to encounter. He used the Black & Peacock Spider and Green Nymph from his original reservoir series together with five patterns that were specifically created for rivers described in this chapter. Three of the flies are variants of standard river patterns and the final two are loosely based on his Green Nymph. They were, like his reservoir nymphs, general representations intended to convey a likeness of the creatures that the trout would expect to see rather than exact imitations of specific insects. The thinking behind their construction was that they should be translucent rather than opaque, have highly mobile hen or game bird hackles, and possess a range of different tone values (the amount of light reflected and transmitted). Although Tom Ivens made the comment that these patterns *'are by no means orthodox'*, they are all flies that G E M Skues would have recognized and they do in fact bear a distinct resemblance to some of Skues' own creations.

G E M Skues' Olive Nymph

   Tom Ivens also fished for sea-trout from time to time and he found that his reservoir nymphs worked just as well as traditional sea-trout flies. His Black & Peacock Spider, which he sometimes dressed for sea-trout with the addition of an oval silver tinsel rib, was highly effective for night time fishing. To demonstrate their versatility his reservoir patterns also accounted for numerous salmon over the years!

Pheasant Tail

Hook: Wet fly hook sizes 12 – 15
Tying thread: Black
Tail: A few cock pheasant centre tail fibres
Body: Reddish brown cock pheasant centre tail fibres, ribbed with fine oval gold tinsel
Thorax: Reddish brown cock pheasant centre tail fibres
Wing case: Reddish brown cock pheasant centre tail fibres
Hackle: One black and one brown hen neck feather wound together as a collar hackle
Head: Tying thread, clear varnished

The PTN is arguably one of the most versatile flies around and it is equally suitable for use on rivers or still waters. Most well-known anglers have made an attempt at designing their own version: G E M Skues, Dr Bell, Frank Sawyer, Oliver Kite and Arthur Cove among them and the above dressing is Tom Ivens' variant.

Tom's pattern is very straightforward in construction but that does not detract from its effectiveness. The concept of tying two different coloured hackle feathers simultaneously is not new but it is a feature that is not encountered all that often nowadays and it does produce an attractive combination in a fly that that could suggest a variety of dayfly nymphs.

March Brown

Hook: Wet fly hook sizes 12 – 15
Tying thread: Black
Tail: Two speckled partridge feather fibres
Body: Hare's ear or guard hairs of rabbit or hare chopped up, ribbed with oval gold tinsel
Hackle: Dark partridge collar hackle
Head: Peacock herl twisted and wound to form a bold head

This is yet another variation of what is probably the most successful and popular general-purpose fly pattern of all time: the Gold Ribbed Hare's Ear. Anglers who settle on just a few flies to cover every eventuality generally have a GRHE of some sort in their fly box.

One of the hallmarks of a classic fly like this is that it can be modified in a variety of ways to replicate a multitude of creatures: an olive nymph, caddis, shrimp or an emerging fly just leaving its shuck – the possibilities are endless. I have always included a hackle on my versions of the GRHE to give it an extra suggestion of life and the mobile partridge hackle on Tom Ivens' tying gives that subtle hint which suggests that it is indeed a living creature.

Neatness in an artificial fly is something that fly dressers strive for but in the case of this pattern it seems that a little roughness only adds to its appeal.

Partridge & Orange

Hook: Wet fly hook sizes 12 – 15
Tying thread: Black
Body: Orange-dyed swan herl, ribbed with fine gold wire
Thorax: Orange-dyed swan herl tied thicker
Wing case: Orange-dyed swan herl
Hackle: Dark partridge collar hackle, fairly long in the fibre
Head: Tying thread, clear varnished

This has long been considered to be an indispensable pattern for fishing the fast-flowing North Country rivers for trout and grayling. Courtney Williams suggests that it serves well as a copy of the February red and also that it could represent a spent spinner, nymph or freshwater shrimp.

Tom Ivens' version is distinctive from the traditional tying as he endeavoured to make it more nymph-like in profile. Flies like this need to be tied with a sparse, mobile hackle and there are few materials in the fly dresser's palette that have the life and suppleness of partridge.

When a fly with a touch of bright colour is needed for it to stand out in that brief instant before it is swept away by the current, or when the water is coloured after rainfall, this pattern takes some beating.

Olive Yellow Nymph

Hook: Wet fly hook sizes 12 – 15
Tying thread: Black
Body: Yellow-dyed and pale green-dyed swan herl in a proportion of 2 to 1 wound simultaneously
Thorax: Yellow-dyed and pale green-dyed swan herl in a proportion of 2 to 1 tied thicker
Wing case: Pale green-dyed swan herl
Hackle: Light partridge collar hackle
Head: Tying thread, clear varnished

The three previous flies are loosely based upon traditional river patterns but this one shows a distinct resemblance to Tom Ivens' Green Nymph from his reservoir series. It is interesting to observe that despite his insistence that slavishly following the exact dressing materials is unnecessary, he nonetheless took the trouble to use yellow and pale-green to achieve the shade he desired in this pattern rather than use a single colour of herl. The effect of blending different materials together can produce that extra sparkle that one colour does not seem to possess.

The profile of this fly is one that Skues would doubtless have been content to use and it will pass muster as a representation of virtually any nymph, larva or crustacean to be found in rivers.

Green Nymph (River Version)

Hook: Wet fly hook sizes 12 – 15
Tying thread: Black
Body: Green-dyed ostrich herl, clipped short after winding to produce a tapered body
Hackle: Dark partridge collar hackle
Head: Peacock herl twisted and wound to form a bold head

As well as using his original reservoir version of the Green Nymph, Tom Ivens also produced this variant which was specifically intended for rivers. It is a much lighter fly which fishes in the upper regions of the water and once again he incorporated a highly mobile partridge feather for the hackle as well as his customary bold peacock herl head.

It makes a pretty fair representation of many of the dayfly nymphs as they move around the river or weed beds; whilst they are ascending to the surface; or else as they drift in the surface film immediately prior to hatching. It can also be pressed into service to replicate a caddis larva, shrimp or some sort of water bug.

The beauty of impressionistic flies like this is that even if you have misjudged the situation, and misread the source of the trout's interest, they could well make a passable copy of the creature the fish are actually targeting!

Chapter 11

REFERENCES TO T C IVENS

Tom Ivens' considerable influence on the development of reservoir fly fishing naturally resulted in numerous published references to him and this chapter reproduces a few (edited) extracts.

A History of Flyfishing
By Conrad Voss Bark, Merlin Unwin Books, Ludlow, Shropshire (1992)
The Legitimate Method
By the time WWII ended most reservoirs had accepted a fly-only rule though some with reservations, but the flies varied considerably. Progress was mainly on the Midland reservoirs where skilled anglers developed new styles and new long distance casting methods.

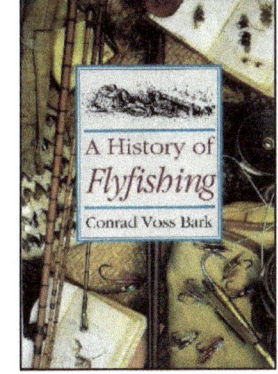

The scene was set for a stillwater code of practice which would provide basic fly patterns and the times and places where they could be used. This came from a Midland angler, T C Ivens, in a book published in 1952 *(Stillwater Fly-Fishing)* which had the same illuminating effect on the reservoirs as Halford's works on the chalkstreams.

Ivens gave details of five standard general patterns which created an impression of certain groups of underwater insects and which could, by representing the trout's natural food, be used for deceiving them. He called these 'deceivers' and they were to be fished slowly.

In contrast, under certain conditions, he advocated the use of 'attractor' patterns, which normally would be fished fast and would provoke the trout into a take. Variations on the theme of these patterns, though not necessarily improvements on them, have continued to be tied ever since.

> Reproduced by kind permission of Merlin Unwin Books

Fly Fishing & Fly Tying Magazine
By Geoffrey Bucknall, Rolling River Publications, Aberfeldy, Perthshire (January 2009)

The Ivens Legacy

If we look back on the pioneers of our sport we notice omissions and mistakes in their methodology. This may be our fault, for we are comparing their work to our own time. We should be making that comparison to their time. To recognize the significance of Tom Ivens' book, *Still Water Fly Fishing*, which was published in the 1960s, we should consider the state of reservoir fly fishing in the post-war era.

What of the man himself? Like many ex-servicemen on low pay he admitted to managing his expenses carefully. He wanted to take advantage of the policy of water authorities to copy the success of Blagdon. Many new reservoirs were stocked with trout. The fishing was made available under a fly-only rule. There was hardly any town or city dweller which did not have access to trout fishing at reasonable cost. This was a revolution, for before the war, in the south and midlands, only a privileged and affluent minority enjoyed trout fishing of that quality.

Ivens knew he had to solve the problem of throwing a long line for he could see the lake floor of the marginal shallows for about 20 yards. He knew he needed to reach 30 yards or more to catch fish. Reading his book today it is clear that he operated within a narrow discipline. It did not seem so at that time. It was revolutionary. I remember that nearly every reservoir addict would own a copy of his book which truly started the post-war development of tactics.

I must refer to the rumours that circulated at that time, that he was not the originator of the book or the fly patterns which bore his name. I do not believe them. Nearly all of them I dismissed; on investigation, they made no sense.

Tom Ivens' time was before the popular explosion of stillwater fly fishing. Without meaning to be, but simply by being a pioneer, he became controversial. His articles, describing his techniques were savagely attacked by Richard Walker in the *Angling Times*, as *'bone-headed athleticism.'* It is bizarre, because later, when Grafham opened on his doorstep, Walker adopted the distance-casting tactics which Tom and myself had introduced, without adding anything new to them, nor crediting his sources, Tom for the double-haul, myself for the light shooting head. In my case, happily Barrie Rickards put the record straight in his biography of Walker. But Barrie did not go into bat for Tom Ivens to whom we reservoir addicts owe a great deal. I hope this article will put right this ancient wrong.

First published in Fly Fishing & Fly Tying *magazine and reproduced by kind permission*

Fishing for Lake Trout
By Conrad Voss Bark, H F & G Witherby, London (1972)
Ivens to Goddard

In 1953, T. C. Ivens published a book on reservoir fishing which has had an important and lasting influence. Ivens was well aware of the conflict between the lure and the fly and tried to resolve this as far as possible in a most practical way. He had discarded all the traditional loch patterns. In their place he simplified the choice of fly to eight simple representations – five of them being nymphs, and one a spider in the Phillips tradition, which could all be fished as deceivers – and the other three being lures which could be fished in circumstances when lure fishing was considered to be most necessary or effective. Among these lures was the now famous Jersey Herd, so called because the original body was tied with the copper foil from the top of a bottle of Jersey milk.

I have great admiration for Ivens. He made an effort to resolve the problem. He established the importance of technique and codified much of the discoveries of the previous ten or twenty years. He tried very hard to establish his preference for nymph fishing over lure fishing, wherever this was possible, and the fact that he failed to do so can be blamed more on the phenomenal success of the Jersey Herd than on his original intention. The Jersey Herd became enormously popular. It still is very popular and is a most effective lure.

By 1971, when the third edition of his book was published, Ivens had almost got to the stage where he felt at times rather regretful that he had designed the Jersey Herd. He had seen the way that lure fishing is abused, the trampling of marginal water, the crowding together, the long casting that drives the trout towards the centre of the lake.

Reproduced by kind permission of Adam Fox-Edwards

Reservoir Trout Flies
By Adrian V W Freer, The Crowood Press, Marlborough (2010)
Tom Ivens
In 1952, Tom Ivens (a nymph fisherman by disposition) introduced the Jersey Herd, one of the first out-and-out flasher lures to gain wide popularity, and thankfully we have a record of why and how it was created in his classic work *Still Water Fly-Fishing,* where he gives an absorbing account of a fly being created to deal with a specific fishing situation.

At the time he attempted to produce a really large, heavy fly which was weighty enough to stay submerged whilst being stripped back quickly in very windy conditions where 'normal' sized flies were far too light and simply skated across the surface. Subsequently, other anglers began to develop similar flashy attractor patterns and 'lure fishing' as we understand it today came into being.

Reproduced by kind permission of The Crowood Press

Chapter 12

PROGRESS Of RESERVOIR FLY FISHING

Reservoir fly fishing has seen many significant changes during the intervening years since Tom Ivens first began to fish Hollowell and Ravensthorpe: stocking policies, the reservoir environment, the trout themselves and predators have become an increasing problem. Despite all these, however, there is little doubt that a Black & Peacock Spider, slowly-recovered in the vicinity of a feeding trout, will still be as effective as ever.

STOCKING POLICIES

In the immediate post-WW2 years the number of trout stocked in reservoirs was very meagre compared with today. At that time anglers could anticipate bags averaging less than one fish, per rod, per day; a figure that would be totally unacceptable nowadays and any water that regularly recorded such low returns would quickly find that their customers had gone elsewhere. These days anglers demand consistent bags and even those with a moderate level of

Stocking with takeable size fish at Eyebrook Reservoir

proficiency expect a few limits each season interspersed with no more than the occasional blank.

As a result of such high expectations, fishery managers now stock much more heavily, very often on a weekly basis, with fish that are already of a takeable size. Whereas in the early post-war years six- to eight-inch trout would be released which would be expected to grow on, nowadays stocking will typically consist of fish of 1½lb upwards with a few larger specimens and even the odd double-figure fish introduced for good measure.

THE RESERVOIR ENVIRONMENT

There is little doubt that the reservoir environment has changed radically in recent times, one of the most noticeable features being the decline in the populations of dayflies and to a lesser extent sedges. Where are the caenis 'blizzards' and the 'mad on' evening rises we once experienced? I know we tend to view the past through rose-tinted spectacles but plainly things are not as they used to be.

Although the reasons for the changes are not entirely clear it would seem that intensive farming methods and the increased use of pesticides, herbicides, fungicides, sheep dip and fertilizers have all played a significant role. These leech out into the watercourses and then into the reservoirs where they are just as efficient at killing aquatic invertebrates as agricultural pests. Today we consume food that is very much 'chemicalized' and we wash fresh produce to get rid of chemicals rather than bugs and creepy-crawlies – when was the last time you encountered a caterpillar when washing salad or vegetables? Steps have been taken to reduce the use of these potent killers and as organic produce becomes more desirable let us pray that we shall see a comeback in aquatic life. It will take time to work through and return to 'normal' but it would be a positive step.

RAINBOWS VERSUS BROWNS

One of the greatest changes to stocking policies has been the switch from browns to rainbows which has occurred for a number of reasons. Rainbow trout grow much faster, are cheaper to rear, they are more active in high water temperatures, being vigorous fish they prune the head of coarse fish more effectively, they rise to surface food more freely and the recovery rate appears to be higher. They are also considered by many to be a nicer-tasting fish.

Nevertheless, despite all these positives the native British brownie is undoubtedly a far more beautiful fish to behold and it is no wonder that it holds a special place in the heart of most fly fishers. As a consequence most managers generally stock at least a few for added interest and, such is their love of these stunning creatures, most anglers tend to return them nowadays.

Two-at-a-time for the author!

TRIPLOID TROUT

Probably the most noteworthy development in fish farming in recent years has been the introduction of triploid brown and rainbow trout. These are in essence sterile fish where the eggs have been modified to retain three chromosomes instead of the customary two (in diploid fish). There are several ways of achieving this; the two most commonly employed methods being heat shocking and pressure treatment of the eggs. Once this procedure has been completed the fish can be hatched, reared and released in the normal way. In practical terms this results in fish that are essentially sexless and as a consequence triploid fish do not expend energy on creating milt or ova but instead concentrate their time on feeding which is transferred into rapid fish growth.

These fish are never 'out of condition' due to spawning and it is claimed by many that the taste and quality of triploid trout flesh is better. From time to time the odd fish will be caught that is packed with ova and presumably the ova treatment did not take effect on that individual fish.

Being unable to interbreed with the resident fish stock, triploids cannot upset the gene pool of the existing population, a risk that can occur with diploid fish. In places where this is a concern it is essential to ensure that all the ova have been treated successfully.

CATCH AND RELEASE

In the early years of reservoir fly fishing the invariable rule was that every fish caught had to be retained. Virtually all fisheries have revised this policy and 'catch and release' is now an option that enables anglers who do not wish to keep their fish to return them. It is a thorny issue with some claiming that many returned fish do not survive (chiefly during warm weather), released trout become hook-shy and consequently harder to catch a second time, and it provides ammunition to the anti-blood sports lobby because we are (allegedly) not treating our quarry with respect. Anglers who keep their catch would maintain that trout are too valuable a 'crop' to be put back, the taste of a freshly-caught reservoir trout beats that of a sad, supermarket one every time, and giving a few trout away to relatives and friends generates positive publicity for the sport.

There are pros and cons on both sides of the argument and it is up to each angler to decide how to act as their conscience dictates.

PREDATORS

Trout fisheries have always suffered from the predation of fish stocks but in recent years it has become an increasingly serious issue. None of the predators mentioned here were a problem in the early post-war years.

The reintroduction of ospreys and otters has led to an increase in predation from them both, although the level of damage they inflict is generally considered to be manageable. They are endangered species and (at the current time) they are only present in small numbers. Nevertheless the situation does need careful monitoring.

The same cannot be said for the black peril – the cormorant! These birds, which are sea birds that have no place inland, routinely consume two pounds of fish flesh, per bird, every single day which equates to the removal of a third of a tonne of fish, per bird, each year. Stocked fish cost a great deal of money to cultivate and when scores of these birds are present it does not take much mathematics to calculate the cost of the damage they cause. Indeed, many rivers and streams are now devoid of silver fish as a result of these ravenous birds. Clearly something needs to be done to rectify the problem and culling would appear to be the only effective solution, although persuading the population at large to agree to kill a bird that is highly visible (although not a particularly attractive one it has to be admitted) in order to protect fish that are to all intents and purposes invisible is easier said than done.

The black peril!

Mink are another worrying problem. Having no natural predator to control their number they rapidly munch their way through the resident fauna and they can decimate an entire locality of animals and birds in no time at all, multiplying in huge numbers in the process, as the incident below demonstrates. Once this happens and the food supply dries up, they eventually die of starvation.

In my coarse fishing days I frequently fished a secluded stretch of the Grand Union Canal and at that time the number of folk who walked the towpath was very small. Sitting quietly, on a regular basis a water vole would scurry to within a yard or so, look me in the eye with surprise and quickly disappear into the water with a 'plop'. It dawned on me one afternoon that these charming little fellows were no longer around, hares that were usually visible in the meadows opposite were absent, and wildfowl and their chicks nowhere to be seen. One day I caught a glimpse of the source of the problem – mink!

Chapter 13

FISHING TACKLE INNOVATIONS BY T C IVENS

As has already been noted, Tom Ivens was at the forefront in the development of reservoir fly fishing tackle. His innovations in fly rods, shooting heads, nets and leaders were all manufactured and sold commercially and in due course became some of the most sought-after items of fishing equipment.

FISHING RODS

He designed a range of two-piece, butt action, split-cane fly rods in conjunction with Davenport & Fordham Ltd. The 1968 range was:
- *'Farstrike'* T C Ivens Original 10ft to cast AFTM DT 6/7 line.
- *'Farstrike'* T C Ivens Lake 10ft to cast AFTM DT 5/6 line.
- *'Farstrike'* T C Ivens Ravensthorpe 9ft 4in to cast AFTM DT 5/6 line.
- *'Farstrike'* T C Ivens Reservoir 9ft 4in to cast AFTM DT 5/6 line.
- *'Farstrike'* T C Ivens *'Superflyte'* 8ft 8in to cast AFTM 7/8 *'Superflyte'* shooting head.

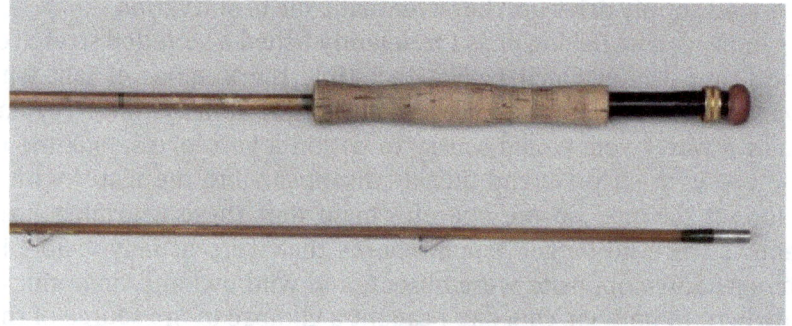

'Farstrike' T C Ivens Ravensthorpe 9ft 4in split-cane fly rod

The split-cane 8ft 8in *'Superflyte'* was superseded in 1970 by a fibre-glass rod:
- *'Farstrike'* T C Ivens *'Ferrulite'* 9ft 10in to cast AFTM 7/8 *'Superflyte'* shooting head.

SHOOTING HEAD FLY LINES

To complement their range of fishing rods, Davenport & Fordham Ltd marketed the *'Superflyte'* series of shooting heads designed in conjunction with Tom Ivens:
- 33ft *'Superflyte'* Floater shooting head AFTM 7, 8, 9 & 10.
- 33ft *'Superflyte'* Sinker shooting head AFTM 7, 8, 9 & 10.
- 100ft *'Superflyte'* shooting head backing.

These were manufactured in the USA by Gudebrod Silk Co and marketed under the *'Farstrike'* brand.

TAPERED NYLON MONOFILAMENT LEADERS

Being able to deliver the flies a long distance is irrelevant if the leader does not turn over and straighten correctly. To facilitate leader turnover Tom Ivens introduced a series of single- and double-tapered nylon monofilament leaders appropriate for a variety of conditions:

- **A.** For general purpose use in normal conditions 11ft: 0.018in tapered to 0.010in (single-taper).
- **B.** For heavy flies in strong and adverse winds 7ft 6in: 0.020in tapered to 0.014in (single-taper).
- **C.** For normal windy conditions 9ft 7in: 0.016in tapered to 0.020in tapered to 0.010in (double-taper).
- **D.** For fishing deep nymphs 14ft: 0.016in tapered to 0.020in tapered to 0.010in (double-taper).
- **E.** For light winds and sunny conditions 11ft 4in: 0.016in tapered to 0.020in tapered to 0.010in (double-taper).

They were based on a series of tapers developed in the United States by Al McClane: two were of McClane's own design and three were Ivens' adaptations intended for English reservoir work.

T C IVENS' FLIES

Tom Ivens' flies were tied and marketed by J J S Walker, Bampton & Co of Alnwick, and Davenport & Fordham Ltd, the latter also selling packets of the correct materials for tying his flies.

FISHING BOAT

Although fishing boats are not normally considered to be an item of fishing tackle, this chapter is perhaps an appropriate place to record Tom Ivens' involvement in their design.

In 1968 Tom Ivens collaborated with Thanetcraft Ltd in the design of the 14ft 3in hand-laid fibre-glass *'Stillwater'* fishing boat for rivers, lakes and the sea which incorporated several unique angling features:

- High seats for a better casting position, well-spaced apart.
- Fixing rings for the mooring ropes, anchors and drogues mounted on the exterior of the hull.
- A snag-free interior to avoid fly line tangles.
- Provision for the oars to be stowed amidships but easily accessible where an outboard engine is fitted.

The 'Stillwater' Boat

The 'Stillwater' *fishing boat manufactured by Thanetcraft*
Image courtesy of Thanetcraft Ltd

As well as requiring a minimum of maintenance the boat possessed two important safety features:
- Built-in buoyancy (600lbs).
- High stability.

Chapter 14

BOOKS AND ARTICLES WRITTEN BY T C IVENS

Listed below are some of his books and articles:

Author:

Still Water Fly-Fishing by T C Ivens:
  First edition, Derek Verschoyle (1952)
  Second edition, André Deutsch (1961)
  Second edition, reprinted with minor revisions, André Deutsch (1963)
  Third edition, revised and enlarged, André Deutsch (1970)
  Third edition, updated (paperback), Pan Books Ltd (1973)
  Fourth edition, revised and enlarged, André Deutsch (1975)

Pond Culture of Food Fishes (thesis) by T C Ivens: Seale-Hayne Agricultural College (c.1952)

First edition

Second edition

Contributor:

The Art of Angling (in three volumes) edited by Kenneth Mansfield (contributor: three articles), Caxton Publishing Co (1957)

The Angler's Year No. 2 edited by Peter Wheat (contributor: one article), Pelham Books (1971)

Third edition

Articles

Tom Ivens contributed articles for a number of angling magazines including:
  Fishing Gazette
  Creel Magazine
  Angling Magazine
  Angler's Annual

Fourth edition

Images courtesy of Welbeck Publishing

Chapter 15

POSTSCRIPT

As we arrive at the conclusion of this survey of Tom Ivens' considerable achievements it is time to summarize his legacy. At a time when reservoir fly fishing was still very much in its infancy he had a huge influence on the direction the sport was taking. His flies were popular, successful and have stood the test of time; the alternative fishing methods he promoted are still employed today; and many of his ground-breaking advances in tackle design are relevant seven decades later. Tom Ivens' place in angling history therefore rests secure.

THE PROGRESS OF RESERVOIR FLY ANGLING

Whilst the advances in fly design undertaken by Dr Bell of Wrington were very considerable, due to his reclusive nature and the fact that he wrote virtually nothing of his exploits much of what he achieved went largely unrecognized and his impact beyond Blagdon was strictly limited[16]. That was certainly not the case with Tom Ivens who, during the 1950s, 1960s and 1970s, was probably the most influential and respected angling figure of the period.

Thankfully, with the publication of *Still Water Fly-Fishing*, the results of his research became available to every angler. Much of what Ivens wrote was truly revolutionary and his scientific approach had an instant appeal. It also spurred later generations of fly anglers to contribute to the advances that anglers benefit from today.

Blagdon Lake and the fishing lodge
Image courtesy of Steve Taylor

That being the case, fly fishers worldwide owe a

debt of gratitude to this forward-thinking angler and his seminal book. Without it many budding anglers who wished to give reservoir fly fishing a try would have had many blank days and perhaps even given up the sport. The fact that these anglers managed to persist and succeed has resulted in reservoir fly fishing becoming one of the largest branches of angling today.

RESERVOIR FLY FISHING IS STILL DEVELOPING

Reservoir fly fishing, like all branches of angling, is in a continual state of development and there have been a great many advances since those introduced by Tom Ivens in the 1950s and the succeeding decades. We now have carbon-fibre fly rods that weigh less than four ounces, free-shooting plastic fly lines that enable long distances to be cast with ease, 'invisible' fluorocarbon leader materials, chemically-sharpened hooks and a vast range of synthetic fly dressing materials. There is also a greater understanding of the food of reservoir trout (and especially the importance of buzzers) and dry fly fishing is now a regular component of the stillwater fly angler's armoury (very much due to the predominance of free-rising rainbows). The list of developments is a long one.

   No doubt in the years to come many of the latest ideas which we currently consider to be ground-breaking will be discarded as irrelevant, but this continual evolution of tackle, flies and techniques must surely be a good and healthy development for the sport.

A RECOMMENDATION

Such is the importance of Ivens' book today that it is still recommended reading for every reservoir fly angler and we are fortunate that (although it is currently out of print) as a result of it being a bestseller numerous reasonably-priced copies are available from second-hand sources. As a textbook detailing a set of techniques to be followed slavishly much of the information may well have been modified or superseded; but as a handbook to guide anglers to *think* the problems through for themselves it remains unsurpassed.

During the preparation of this current volume it has been both fascinating and enlightening to read the four editions side-by-side to discover what information has remained, been modified, taken out or added and this is a demonstration of the way in which reservoir fly anglers constantly hone their understanding in the light of experience. It takes time, determination, enthusiasm and hard work to master any worthwhile discipline and fly fishing is no different, but the gradual accumulation of angling skills and knowledge is all part of the fascination that makes angling the absorbing, compelling and unique pursuit it is. As Tom Ivens once remarked, 'there is certainly much more to fly fishing than killing fish!'

Tom Ivens with a four-fish limit of Hollowell trout
Image courtesy of the Ivens family

CONCLUDING THOUGHTS

Fly anglers are privileged to be able to participate in what is undoubtedly the most glorious sport known to mankind. Every time we go out there are new sights to be admired, delightful creatures to observe, etiquette to be followed, problems to be solved, frustrations to overcome and at the end of the day the most beautiful, stunning and enigmatic creature in the world as our quarry. It is no wonder that after a day's fishing we sleep all the better for it.

With those concluding thoughts may I wish you safe and happy days at the waterside, convivial fishing companions, tight lines, screaming reels and may your tying thread never break!

NOTES

Chapter 1

1. Scientists classify lakes into three main categories: eutrophic meaning 'well nourishing', these are shallow and rich in bottom feed and typical of lowland reservoirs built on fertile land; oligotrophic meaning 'little nourishing' and are characteristic of deep lakes where bottom feed is restricted and surface food more important; and dystrophic meaning 'badly nourishing' which are stained by peat and other organic matter and are acidic, if they do contain trout the stock will be few in number and small in size and they are therefore of little interest to fly anglers.

Chapter 2

2. Arthur Cove in *My Way with Trout*.
3. Bob Church in *Reservoir Trout Fishing*.
4. To the great loss of the sport, Cyril Inwood sadly died of a heart attack in 1971 at the early age of 59.
5. Alan Pearson in *Trout Angler's Angles*.
6. The dustjacket text of the first (1952) edition of *Still Water Fly-Fishing* reads as follows: *'More often than not, the competent river angler when visiting a lake finds his gear and methods useless, and the end of the day sees him 'clean', watching the local experts weigh in sizeable fish* taken by methods which they guard as secrets. *Here a specialist in lake fishing places at the disposal of novice and expert alike the experience gained in many years of specialization in lake fishing'* (emphasis mine).
7. Steve Parton in *The Fly-School Notes*.

Chapter 3

8. The flies recommended by Bridgett include: (nymphs) Olive Nymph, Green Nymph and Black Nymph; (imitative flies) March Brown Spider, Red Palmer, Blae & Black, Corncrake Sedge*, Cinnamon Sedge*, Woodcock & Yellow, Blae & Yellow, Greenwell's Glory*, Medium Olive and Rough Olive*; (attractor lures) Peter Ross, Butcher, Grouse & Claret and Teal & Green.
*May be fished dry together with the Blue Hen Spider and Badger Hackle.
9. The chalk streams are located in Hampshire and the surrounding counties and possess some of the finest and most sought-after trout fishing in England, and indeed the world. They include the Avon, Itchen, Test, Frome, Kennet and their tributaries. They are renowned for the size and quality of their fish.

10. Frederic M Halford (1844-1914) was a highly influential fly angler, entomologist and author. Halford (in conjunction with George Marryat 1840-1896) devised and promoted the use of dry flies on the southern chalk streams. He was much acclaimed during his lifetime but his dogmatic approach, stipulating the use of the 'dry fly only' at all times when other methods such as Skues' nymph techniques would be more effective, led to considerable criticism after his death.

11. G E M Skues (1858-1949) was a leading fly angler and author who has been described as 'the father of nymph fishing'. It was Skues who challenged the fixation with the 'dry fly only' conventions prevalent on the southern chalk streams. Despite the fact that his creations were imitations of the trout's food, albeit imitations of *subsurface* food, he received a great deal of unwarranted condemnation and criticism from purists. He had a great influence on Dr Bell of Wrington who applied his methods to reservoirs. History has since exonerated Skues but it is sad that he received such antagonism during his lifetime.

12. The term 'purist' is used alternatively as one of commendation or denigration of fly fishers. The definition given by Halford is as follows: *'Those of us who will not in any circumstances cast except over rising fish are sometimes called ultra-purists and those who will occasionally try to tempt a fish in position, but not actually rising, are styled purists.'*

Chapter 5

13. Frank Sawyer (1907-1980) was the keeper on the River Avon for sixty years. He was largely responsible for the development of modern river nymph fishing using leaded patterns for subsurface-feeding trout. His most widely known pattern is his Pheasant Tail Nymph.

Chapter 6

14. Research carried out by the author for *Dr Bell's Trout Flies* unearthed Dr Bell's similar Black Peacock Nymph which came many years before the Black & Peacock Spider. There is little doubt that other flies utilizing a black hackle and peacock herl body were created prior to the B&P of which there is no known record. It was Ivens, however, who popularized the fly.

Chapter 9

15. Since then Rutland Water at 3,100 acres opened in 1976, and Kielder Water at 2,680 acres in 1981.

Chapter 15

16. This omission has been remedied with the publication of two recent books by the author: *Dr Bell of Wrington* and *Dr Bell's Trout Flies* (see bibliography).

BIBLIOGRAPHY

Books

Bridgett, R C. *Loch-Fishing in Theory and Practice*. Herbert Jenkins, London, 1924.
Bucknall, Geoffrey. *Fly-Fishing Tactics on Still Water*. Frederick Muller, London, 1966.
Cove, Arthur. *My Way with Trout*. The Crowood Press, Marlborough, Wiltshire, 1986.
Freer, Adrian V W. *Reservoir Trout Flies*. The Crowood Press, Marlborough, Wiltshire, 2010.
Freer, Adrian V W. *Dr Bell of Wrington*. Welford Court Press, Oadby, Leicestershire, 2019.
Freer, Adrian V W. *Dr Bell's Trout Flies*. Coch-y-Bonddu Books, Machynlleth, Powys, 2020.
Frost, W E & Brown, M E. *The Trout*. Collins, London, 1967.
Halford, Frederic M. *Floating Flies and How to Dress Them*. Sampson Low, Marston, Searle, and Rivington, London, 1886.
Halford, Frederic M. *Dry-Fly Fishing in Theory and Practice*. Sampson Low, Marston, Searle, and Rivington, London, 1889.
Ivens, T C. *Still Water Fly-Fishing: A Modern Guide to Angling in Reservoirs and Lakes*. Derek Verschoyle, London, 1952.
Macan, T T & Worthington, E B. *Life in Lakes and Rivers*. Bloomsbury Books, London, 1951.
Mansfield, Kenneth (editor). *The Art of Angling*. Caxton Publishing, London, 1957.
Sawyer, Frank. *Nymphs and the Trout*. A & C Black, London, 1958.
Skues, G E M. *Minor Tactics of the Chalk Stream*. A & C Black, London, 1910.
Skues, G E M. *The Way of a Trout with a Fly*. A & C Black, London, 1921.
Voss Bark, Conrad. *A History of Flyfishing*. Merlin Unwin Books, Ludlow, Shropshire, 1992.

Voss Bark, Conrad & Restall, Eric. *The New Encyclopaedia of Fly Fishing*. Robert Hale, London, 1999.
Voss Bark, Conrad. *Fishing for Lake Trout*. H F & G Witherby, London, 1972.
Walker, C F. *Lake Flies and their Imitation*. Herbert Jenkins, London, 1960.

Articles

Bucknall, Geoffrey. *The Ivens Legacy.* Fly Fishing & Fly Tying magazine, January 2009.
Freer, Adrian V W. *Tom Ivens' River Patterns.* Flydresser journal, Summer 2021.
Huffer, Mick. *Tying and Fishing the Black & Peacock Spider.* Fly Fishing & Fly Tying magazine, September 2009.

Websites

T C Ivens: www.webdatauk.wixsite.com/t-c-ivens
Coch-y-Bonddu Books: www.anglebooks.com
Dr Bell of Wrington: www.webdatauk.wixsite.com/dr-bell
Fly Dressers' Guild: www.flydressersguild.org
Fly Fishing & Fly Tying magazine: www.flyfishing-and-flytying.co.uk
The Seale-Haynians (Alumni) Club: www.seale-hayne.com

Quotations by T C Ivens

'I have always attempted to elevate fishing to the plane of an exact science.'

'The man who thinks 'fish and fishing' must ultimately succeed in catching more fish.'

'We must try to think like our quarry, the trout.'

'To be wrong in one thing is to be suspected of fallibility in all things.'

'Part of the fun of fly fishing is the gradual accumulation of the necessary skills. There is certainly much more to fly fishing than killing fish!'

THE AUTHOR

Adrian Freer was born, and still lives, in Leicestershire and was educated at Loughborough Grammar School and Leicester College of Art & Technology (now De Montfort University). He is married with two daughters and four grandchildren.

He started fishing as a boy in the 1950s, in the days when the Leicester Canal was producing its memorable catches, and caught his first trout on an artificial fly from Eyebrook Reservoir in the early 1960s.

Initially, Adrian was mainly a coarse fish angler and participated in numerous matches, but for the last thirty years he has fished almost exclusively for trout, fishing the large Midlands reservoirs. A dedicated fly fisherman and fly tyer, he also has a keen interest in entomology and angling history.

Adrian Freer is the author of a number of books including the highly acclaimed *Successful Reservoir Fly Fishing Techniques* (2007), *Reservoir Trout Flies* (2010), *A Biblical Defence of the Sport of Angling* (2016), *Dr Bell of Wrington* (2019) and *Dr Bell's Trout Flies* (2020). He also contributes articles for *Fly Fishing & Fly Tying* magazine and *Flydresser* journal.

In addition to fly fishing his other interests include church activities, music, foreign travel and writing.

Visit his website: www.webdatauk.wixsite.com/adrian-freer

INDEX

Alexandra 51
Art of Angling 18, 55, 91
attractors 15, 31, 79, 82
bank fishing 29, 33
Bell, Dr 27-29, 36, 38
Bell's Bug 38
birds 54, 56, 72, 87
Black & Peacock Spider 25, 43-44, 73, 83
Black Knight 64
Black Knight Tandem Streamer 67
Blagdon Buzzer Nymph (Bell) 15, 38
Blagdon Lake 27, 28, 92
boat fishing 27, 29
Bridgett, R C 27, 95
Brooke, Rev Charles 54
Brown & Green Nymph 19, 48
Brown Nymph 46
brown trout 84-85
Bucknall, Geoffrey 34, 80-81
buzzer 47, 60-61

caenis 84
catch and release 86
Chew Valley Lake 14
chironomids 47
Church, Bob 21
Cinnamon & Gold 62
cormorant 87
Cove, Arthur 21
Crane Fly 66

Daddy Long Legs 66
dapping 66
Davenport & Fordham 17, 88-90
deceivers 15, 31-32

Dr Bell's Trout Flies 29
Drury, Col Esmond 38
dry fly fishing 52, 93
'dry fly only' 96
Durleigh Reservoir 14
dystrophic 95

Encyclopaedia of Fly Fishing 20
entomology 19
eutrophic 95
evening rise 36, 84
'exact imitation' – see imitation
Eyebrook Reservoir 21, 22, 83

fertilizers 84
fibre-glass 17, 35, 89, 90
fishery manager 84, 85
Fishing for Lake Trout 81-82
Fishing Gazette 14, 16, 38
flashers 15, 31-32, 37, 82
fly dressing 37-40
Fly Fishing & Fly Tying 80-81
fly line 17, 33, 35, 89
Freer, Adrian V W 82
Fuzzy Buzzy 52

Gentile 38, 59
Grafham Water 57, 71-72
Green & Yellow Nymph 47
Green Nymph 45, 73
Green Nymph (River Version) 78

hackle configurations 39
Hair Wing Butcher 65
Halford, F M 30, 96
History of Flyfishing 79-80
Hollowell Reservoir 14, 29, 55-56
hook scales 39-40
hook sizes 39-40

imitation 15, 27, 28, 30
invasive species 71, 87
Inwood, Cyril 21-22, 24-25
Ivens Orchids 14
Ivens, Ruth 12, 20
Jersey Herd 50, 81-82
Killer Bug (Sawyer) 38
Ladybower Reservoir 21
Lake District 26
Lineham, Cyril 20
Loch Leven 26
long casting 17, 33-34, 81
maggot 59
mammals 55, 56, 72
March Brown 75
McAlpine Ltd, Sir Robert 14
McClane, Al 89
Mid-Northants Trout Fishers' 16
mink 87
Muddler Minnow 69
Northampton 12, 13, 20
Northampton school 22, 23, 24
oligotrophic 95
Olive Nymph (Skues) 73
Olive Yellow Nymph 77
osprey 54, 56, 72, 86
otter 55, 56, 86
Partridge & Orange 76
Pearson, Alan 22
Pennell scale 39-40
pesticides 84
Pheasant Tail 74
pike 14, 55
Pitsford 13, 20
Polar Bear 63
predators 30, 86, 87
Pretty Pretty 49
purist 30, 96
railways 26

rainbow trout 84-85, 93
Ravensthorpe Reservoir 14, 27, 29, 53-55
recovery speeds 35-36
Redditch scale 40
Reservoir Trout Flies 82
rods 17, 35, 88-89, 93
Royal Navy 12
salmon 18, 31, 73
Sawyer, Frank 38, 96
Seale-Hayne College 13
sea-trout 18, 73
sedge 84
sheep dip 84
shooting head 17, 34-35, 89
Skues, G E M 28, 30, 73, 96
specimen fish 44, 55, 67, 71, 84
split-cane 17, 88
Sticky Willy 70
Still Water Fly-Fishing 16, 23-25
'Stillwater' boat 18, 90
stocking policies 19, 83-84
tandem 44, 67
trigger points 38-39
triploid 85-86
trolling 69, 72
Veal's of Bristol 38
Voss Bark, Conrad 20, 79-80, 81-82
Wadham, John 19-20
Walker, Bampton & Co 90
Walker, Richard 16-17, 81
Whisky Fly 68
Whisky Muddler 69
wildlife 54-55, 56, 72, 87
Williams, Courtney 76
WW1 27
WW2 12, 14, 29
zander, record 72

Also in the Fly Fishing Heritage Series: Number One

DR BELL OF WRINGTON: PIONEER OF RESERVOIR FLY FISHING

By Adrian V W Freer

This book is dedicated to the life, the artificial flies, the pioneering techniques in stillwater nymph fishing and ultimately the angling legacy of Dr Howard Alexander Bell (1888-1974) of Wrington, Somerset. Dr Bell regularly fished Blagdon Lake in the years following WW1 where he sought to devise better methods of catching reservoir trout.

As a result of his enquiring and scientific mind Dr Bell did not follow the standard practice of the day by employing traditional patterns but instead he studied the creatures that the fish were targeting and endeavoured to design artificial patterns which replicated them, and retrieved them in a manner which mimicked their progression through the water.

He was probably the first angler to implement such an approach to reservoirs and his Blagdon Buzzer Nymph is the forerunner of the multitude of buzzer artificials employed today.

Includes 95 photographs and 5 maps

Published by Welford Court Press ISBN 978-1-7985301-4-6

Distributed by Amazon Fulfilment

www.ingramcontent.com/pod-product-compliance
Lightning Source LLC
Chambersburg PA
CBHW071724040426
42446CB00011B/2207